Michael Tortorello

LIVE LIKE YOU ARE DYING

DYING

Spiritual Lessons for a Lifetime

Live Like You Are Dying

LIVE LIKE YOU ARE DYING

Spiritual Lessons for a Lifetime

By Michael Tortorello

TORT PUBLISHING LLC

Glastonbury, CT

Edited by Adam Tortorello

Additional editing by Heidi Ragsdale of Text Perfected

DISCLAIMER

Life is precious, and this book in no way implies that a person should choose their death over their life. This book encourages faith, hope, and embracing the beauty of life and does not recommend suicide.

Dedication

This book is dedicated to Kathy, Adam, Melissa, Joseph, Jennifer, Lauren, and Ryan.

Their lives helped inspire my writing of this book.

Live Like You Are Dying

Michael Tortorello

Table of Contents

Introduction...1

CHAPTER 1 Just Died..5

CHAPTER 2 Spiritual Lessons and Spiritual Virtues.......................23

CHAPTER 3 The Law of Attraction and the Spiritual Law of

Attraction..43

CHAPTER 4 Meditation...57

CHAPTER 5 Balance and Spiritual Balance....................................71

CHAPTER 6 Self-doubt and Our Spirit.......................................83

CHAPTER 7 Higher Consciousness...99

CHAPTER 8 Synchronicity and Spiritual Synchronicity....................105

CHAPTER 9 Oneness and Universal Oneness..................................117

CHAPTER 10 The Spirit of Intuition and Clairvoyance.....................131

CHAPTER 11 Health and Supreme Spiritual Health.........................143

CHAPTER 12 Love and Spiritual Love......................................157

CHAPTER 13 Happiness..175

CHAPTER 14 Jesus Christ and Multiple Religions..........................193

CHAPTER 15 Conclusion: Death and Life's Purpose........................207

Works Cited..217

About the Author..223

Live Like You Are Dying

Introduction

This is a personal growth book specifically designed to help you find success and happiness through positive thinking, greater mental awareness, and spiritual growth. One of my goals is to shed light on the age-old questions man has asked himself since the beginning of time, "Why are we humans on this planet, and does life have a purpose?" I contend that we are all here for a purpose. Life is not meaningless or accidental. I will have you explore the purpose or meaning of your personal life.

By taking a holistic approach to body, mind, and spirit, I will show you how to find supreme personal health. This book will provide you with tools to keep you physically healthy and also improve your self-esteem and build your confidence. You will develop your Spiritual Senses including intuition, insight, creativity, imagination, and awareness. You will become a fantastic problem solver. You will learn and practice spiritual lessons of the Universe that will improve your existence forever.

This book will help you find a profession that you are passionate about. The ideas in this book are highly likely to bring you prosperity and an abundance of riches. These riches include peace, happiness, and success in life, which can all be achieved by tapping into your authentic, spiritual self. This book will prepare you to find true love and better understand your current or future soulmate. Practicing the exercises in this book will help you relieve anxiety and avoid depression.

Your newfound achievements and joy will be discovered when the book teaches you how to direct your thought process towards positive ideas, increased mental awareness, and higher consciousness. You will learn that by practicing spiritual virtues, you will love others more deeply, spread kindness, and become more generous and grateful. In return, the Universe will return these virtues to you, but in much greater quantity. As you allow this book to connect you with the Divine Energy Source or God, you will have the spiritual support needed to avoid all failures, resulting in your happiness and success.

You will learn the importance of thinking about your inevitable death. Instead of knowing that you should 'live each day like it may be your last,' you will be taught practical techniques (such as meditation) on how to actually appreciate all your life moments. Your fears of death will diminish, and you will begin to cherish and take advantage of each daily breath of life.

You may have read self-help, self-improvement, or personal growth books. I know that I have probably read more than a hundred of these types of books over the past forty years. Many of these books have given me practical tools and information that have enriched my life with joy and success. I hope my knowledge will be concisely imparted to you so that you may have this same joy and success.

This book is unique because I use both fictional and nonfictional forms of creative writing. Nonfictional books sometimes become banal and repetitive, and I felt that by adding some fiction, I could spice up this personal growth book for a better reader experience. I trust that the fictional part of the book will stimulate your imagination, creativity, passion, and Godlike nature, as you learn that you are One with all people, nature, and the Spiritual Universe.

This book is also different because most personal growth books do not discuss in detail Divine Energy and life after death. The point will clearly be made that I feel noticeably confident about the existence of life after death and how this level of consciousness will manifest. You, the reader, will be imaginatively brought into the Afterlife where you will experience how it feels and what it looks like. You will then be brought back to Earth, where you will live a better life having experienced your own imaginative demise.

I have recently been learning a little about artificial intelligence. We have an Amazon Echo Spot in my house and one morning I asked Alexa simply out of curiosity, "Alexa, are you getting smarter?" Her response was, "I am learning to be more helpful to as many people as possible." Surprised by her astute answer, I said to myself, "Wouldn't it be lovely if we all made that one of our goals in life, to help as many people as possible?" I thought to myself that this is a major reason I am writing this book. If my book can help just a few people become happier, more successful, or more loving, I would be elated. When my readers learn that their physical mortality is less important than their spiritual growth and relationship to Divine Energy, then I have succeeded. When you actualize that spiritual energy of the Universe, and your connectedness to the Divine Energy Source or God elevates your journey to a euphoric eternal life, then my purpose has been realized. By experiencing your true identity, which is your spiritual self, all things will become possible for you. Furthermore, it is my sincere hope that by experiencing the Spirit of the Divine Universe, you will come to believe through faith that death is an illusion and that we all will live together and forever in heavenly bliss.

Live Like You Are Dying

CHAPTER 1
Just Died

Why don't human beings, who are the Lord of all creation, have wings? Is it enough that people live limited to the earth? Actually, we have higher-dimensional wings. Once you die and shed your physical body, you will fly.

—Sun Myung Moon

It is natural to die as to be born.

—Francis Bacon

My New Afterlife

I am in a funeral parlor in Connecticut. I am lying dead in my casket. I died recently. A long time before dying, I told my significant other and my kids that I just wanted to be cremated and put in an urn after I die. I guess they wanted to have the service for me anyway. I certainly hope they won't bury me in the ground because I am still afraid of this.

My family, who initiated my wake, came to see me the first night I was laid out. They were extremely sad, and I could see tears in their eyes. Even though I was dead, I could feel their extreme sorrow and love for me. Fortunately, I had already told my children many times prior to my demise how much I loved them. I did not feel any regrets about the way I had treated them and did not feel there was something I should have told them prior to my death.

As I hovered above them, I began to think about my life. I thought about mistakes I had made and wished I had done a few things differently when I was alive. I guess I did have some regrets after all. I wondered what I could've done differently to make my life easier, more fun, and more peaceful. Could I have been happier? I certainly did not fulfill all the dreams and desires I had when I was younger. Why was that? I thought about the really happy times in my life, like when my children were born. I also thought about many of the lows in my life, including my marital divorces, my times without enough money, the ten years of smoking cigarettes, and the brief period when I experimented with drugs.

I was soon lifted up higher by the Universal spirit force of the Universe where I found myself on a new plane of existence. My mortal self had been transformed into a new living entity that was more Godlike. With the power rush of an enlightened Universe and Universal Knowledge, answers permeated my entire being. I was about to gain spiritual knowledge that would teach me and all those listening important lessons regarding a better way to approach human living.

You might be wondering where I am now, since I said I am dead. Well, I am on a continuous spiritual adventure. After all, is not every one of our lifetimes an adventure? It is no different this time. The players change and the surroundings change, but it is still an adventure. I did not start as a baby this time. Instead, I started as an adult being. I have no distinct physical body currently. There are no time and space limitations here. Communication among the souls here in the Afterlife is rarely performed using language, but there is communication, nevertheless. Sometimes I find myself in more than one place at a time. It is like I am being consistently cloned, but not exactly. There is no experience like this on Earth.

Now, to the human mind, a lack of physical form and no limitations to time and space may seem difficult to imagine, but I assure you that to myself and all the other souls here, this is completely natural. I would not say we fly per se, but we certainly do transport through time and space. You can think of it as dreaming, so that you can relate to my experience. In dreams, you find yourself in situations and settings wherein you usually do not know how you got there. Things happen in dreams that would be impossible in real life. You may see your mother's face on someone else's body, for instance. In the dream, you may be in Los Angeles and then find yourself lost in New York City moments later. You may see everything in black and white and find yourself trying to tell someone (and you are not sure whom) that something important is about to happen, but you cannot get the words out of your mouth. In our dreams, we are not confined to our physical body or limited by the physical properties on Earth. Here in the Afterlife, you may transport yourself or go back in time if you wish. You can even cross back over to see the living occasionally.

There is a lot more freedom in this Afterlife. There are also fewer rules, and I enjoy this. There are very few worries of physical sickness because there is no body to become ill. Imagine a world without insurance premiums or co-pays. Not bad, right? I do not think there is an atmosphere here, although sometimes I see reflections off what looks like gases. I have not been able to detect any wind yet. This calm atmosphere would make for a very pleasant round of golf, but I am not even sure if there is gravity.

One of the greatest aspects of this place is that everything is so simple. When I first arrived, I was genuinely concerned about what I would do for finances. I remembered that when I was alive, I struggled with how to save money for my future. I was often concerned that a check would bounce or I would not have enough money for all the things that my children might need. As I got older, I was not certain I would have enough money for retirement. There was so much apprehension about making my retirement plans.

Upon arrival, I was told by deeply knowledgeable souls, who I could hardly visualize due to their lack of form, "You should put 70% of your money in the S&P 500 index ETF or a similar mutual fund. Keep the other 30% nearby for essentials, incidentals, and emergency use. This system of asset allocation works like a charm." Incredible! Just as I was thinking this sounded like Earth, they laughed and said, "We are just kidding. There is no money up here in this life." I thought to myself, "Certainly, humor has not been lost in the Afterlife." I soon learned that there were no dollars, euros, or Bitcoin needed. In fact, if money were needed, you could desire it with your thoughts, and the abundance of the Universe would grant it to you. Venmo accounts have been replaced by people chanting the Biblical phrase, "Ask and you shall receive."

It seems like most things are just this simple in my Afterlife. Anything I want or need, I can obtain by starting with my intention. In this way, thoughts become things. When I was on Earth, I could have been doing this too, but I hardly ever put enough effort into it. When alive, I never thought I knew enough about business to become wealthy. Although later in life I had a comfortable monetary lifestyle, my wealth was certainly limited by my restricted thinking. I always believed that the harder I worked, the more successful I could become. People told me this my entire life. It turns out that working as hard as one can will get you by, but rarely do you obtain wealth in this way. Working 'smartly' is more important than doing arduous work. I used to see myself as someone who would never own an estate, and certainly not a vacation home, a BMW, or a yacht.

Have you ever seen the classic Christmas movie *It's a Wonderful Life*, featuring Donna Reed and Jimmy Stewart? Do you remember Clarence, the angel in the movie who is trying to earn his wings? Well, Clarence is up here with me right now. He asked me, without words of course, "How did you ever expect to have a vacation home, BMW, or a yacht, if you saw yourself as someone who would never have those things?" At that moment I felt stupid, even though I do not think stupidity exists here. On Earth, I had already conditioned my conscious mind and subconscious mind to believe I would never have these luxury items. Therefore, I would never go through the process of concentrating on getting them or feel the glory of having them. I also never visualized how wonderful I would look with them. In essence, I never opened myself up to having them. The Universe was giving me signs and clues to help me see how they could easily become mine, but I was closed off to the symbols created by the Universe.

Here in the Afterlife, Universal principles and power are obvious and omniscient. There is no physical body or physical world holding me back.

Here, I am in touch with both my authentic self and my intuitive, spiritual self. With my soul functioning on a spiritual level, all my desires are actualized. Because my intentions and beliefs are righteous and I have complete faith in the outcome, all my desires become my reality. Now I have all the wonderful things I ever wanted, so I asked Clarence, "Am I in heaven? Am I with God?" "Not yet," Clarence responds with a devilish grin.

There is another angel who visits me from time to time. Her name is Claribel. I can intuitively sense Claribel is about twenty-eight Earth years old. Although her physical form is not clear, I am able to tell that she is stunning, but I have no idea how I know this. Her hourglass silhouette shimmers in the light for a split second and then wavers out of focus. Her diffuse gaseous supernatural form radiates Venus-like spiritual beauty. I am not sure how I understand how beautiful she is, but I intuitively comprehend her attractiveness. Her form radiates soothing warmth and angelic illumination. When Claribel comes to visit me, I feel nothing but love.

Now, you may wonder about love here in the Afterlife, and I can tell you that everyone who wants to have true love does. It is not something that you have when you first get here. There is a process that you go through, which quickly and easily finds your soulmate. You are told that you must like yourself first. The next stage is to love yourself. Since our souls are inherently pure, we release this purity into our higher consciousness.

We feel our integrity, honesty, love, gratefulness, and kindness emerge from our souls and penetrate our total existence. We now know we are filled with goodness and Godliness. At this moment, we both like and love ourselves. We know that we are a giving entity who is now capable of sharing love, mercy, and gratitude with others. Finding another with desirable physical attributes becomes less important than possessing inner spiritual virtues. We long for someone blessed with the aforementioned virtues. We now know that the Universe will deliver to us the entity that will be our soulmate forever. We start to believe that our soulmate has already been found. We feel their love and caring, prior to even meeting them. We begin to feel the sensations of kindness, goodness, and love that they transmit to us before we ever meet. I visualized how splendid and radiant that perfect loving soul is before our encounter. Finally, she appears, and I intuitively know this is my perfect soulmate, and we merge as one. We are both capable of being separate individual souls, but we can also be a merged, loving soul, coupled in loving energy. This relationship is a facet of Universal Oneness.

I think about why I had so much trouble finding my one soulmate on Earth. I know that mostly the obstacle was my ego self. In the human form, I had many self-doubts. I often lacked self-confidence. I also was not sure of who I wanted, exactly. I often thought that this person needed to be tall and thin, with blond hair and a nice figure. The woman needed to be educated, intelligent, and of course, have an excellent job. I certainly did not want a negative person with several hang-ups. Paradoxically, I was short and plump. I certainly was far from perfect, and yet I was looking for the perfect woman. In my pursuit to find a mate, I would sometimes meet some nice, kind women, but because they did not fit into my pigeonholes, I looked right past them. Sometimes, while I was alive, the Universe would try to send me signs and clues to direct me on the correct path to find my soulmate. The Universe, usually through synchronicity, would have that woman enter my life. Unfortunately, for my first 60 years, I was too blind to follow the signs and allow that woman a chance to show me the perfect match they could become. Sometimes, I would not try the new dating site because it was just another expense, or I was tired of trying online dating. That turned out to be a lost opportunity. Sometimes, I felt too tired to go to the party or lacked the energy to go to a dance. These are examples of the opportunities I missed to meet my soulmate. Then, at age 52, I found a woman with a great-sounding profile on Match.com. She even lived in my town! She did not respond to me, but seven years later, I saw her profile on a new dating site called Our Time. I kept an open mind, and when I texted her this time, she communicated back to me. I realized that seeing her pictures on a different website many years later was not random but rather a synchronicity, given to me by the Universe as an invitation for a second chance at love. She has become my significant other and is now my soulmate.

You may wonder if there is work in the Afterlife. You are probably thinking, "There must be work because you have so much time on your hands." "You have to do something," you say. On Earth, we worked to make a living. When I was alive, I worked hard for over forty years. But remember, here in the Afterlife, we have all the money we could ever need, which is none. Any work becomes a labor of love. This means we only do the work that we love to perform. The Universe here tells us that we should only work at things we are passionate about. We should work so we can learn about the important spiritual principles of existence, whether in the Afterlife or in our life on Earth. We learn in the Afterlife to work at giving service to others. We learn the spiritual lessons of love and communication with Divine Energy or God, and we turn potential goodness into enhancing life's virtues. We work on learning spiritual lessons still not achieved in past lives. We work because it makes us feel good, accomplished, and happy. We never work extremely hard because there is no reason to allow work to be painful. Before work becomes painful, we stop and move on to work that is fun and makes us happy. We never stay in a job longer than we should. On Earth, I always stayed in jobs too long. In time, this became a detriment to my professional growth. If we do not know what new work to do, we ask the power of the Universe, and it gives us clues and signs as to the work we will become passionate about. Here, we do not dismiss the clues and signs because we are open to the answers the world is always giving us. We begin to believe the perfect job will come our way. We never entertain the idea we will not find this job. We visualize ourselves as already having the new job and feeling happy in this new work. In this way, we begin to feel the love and passion of this toil. The Law of Attraction tells us that thoughts become things. With intention, we visually imagine desirable work coming to us. While experiencing the wonderful feeling of already possessing a job we are passionate about, we ultimately receive the work.

Those of us who, like myself, have crossed over, are dead to Earthlings; but I am very much alive in a fully celestial spiritual world. There are no televisions, computers, or smart phones here because there is no need for any of these. There is, however, aesthetic art and ethereal music. Communication is effortless and efficient as there are no faxes, copy machines, emails, downloads, or uploads required. Meditation is a state of mind instead of a forced exercise. Our normal state of consciousness is *higher consciousness*, assimilated and cultivated as absolute concentration and pure awareness of all thoughts, events, and emotions. We are all one-hundred percent mindful, day and night. By virtue of our eternal enlightenment, we have peace and calmness. There are no sports, and for you Harry Potter fans, there is no Quidditch. There are no cars, trains, or planes, because we all use our cognizance to transport us to desired locations.

There is no such thing as being in your physical body anymore. You are your higher consciousness, which is a state of spiritual mind. There are no teeth to brush, no hair to cut or comb, and no nails to clip. There is also no body to become disheveled and decayed in senescence. Sickness and pain are a glum reality of the mortal world, but bliss and fulfillment are harvested in our world. As in Buddhist philosophy, the ego's divisive attachments have been nearly eliminated. Our communication with others is enhanced through an exchange of kinship with the Oneness of all entities. We are all connected to each other and to the spiritual sanctity of the Universe as we slowly march toward God's Kingdom.

Grass, trees, mountains, rivers, and streams are not routinely visualized, although we sometimes conjure up all of nature when we desire. Many of us like to become One with nature. When we pray to God, there are no longer shirts, dresses, shoes, hats, or accessories to these garments. For those who love to shop, I apologize to you ahead of your death.

Money is nonexistent, but we all are rich beyond our dreams. You might be starting to say to yourself that this Afterlife sounds boring and not fun at all. After all, there are no wonderful foods to enjoy, no technology (which eliminates Facebook and Instagram), no clothes, no shopping, no sports, and no cars or airplanes.

Let me address the marvel and wonderment of the Afterlife. No one ever becomes ill, and no one ever dies! Your next transformation will only bring you to a more advanced level of all-knowing enlightenment as you advance toward eternal life with God. There is no physical suffering or mental illness. No one ever cries, as we are almost always filled with positive emotions. We experience the virtues of love, righteousness, mercy, prudence, courage, justice, hope, charity, faith, joy, kindness, and thankfulness. Most of the spirits here are free from self-doubt (insecurity), fear, and worry. It is only those beings who are still struggling with one or two spiritual lessons who may still have some fears or worries. This, however, is unusual. Almost exclusively, total and complete contentment and happiness are aligned with the higher consciousness. We have become omnipresent (present everywhere at the same time), omnipotent (with unlimited power to do anything), and omniscient (all-knowing) in the image of God. There is no jealousy, greed, anger, hatred, violence, judgment, or evil of any kind.

Death's Relationship to Life

The way we live may determine the way we die. The paradox is that our death on Earth can teach us how to live. Those who have had near-death experiences unanimously tell us of a wonderful warm feeling when they left their bodies and began to transform into the Afterlife. The dead tell us they are greeted by warm, loving spirits, who had previously passed on. Some of these are their family members. They experience tunnels and bright lights. More importantly, almost all of them come away with three common themes:

1. There is life after death.

2. Death is not to be feared.

3. After they are told it isn't their time to go and are sent back to Earth, they learn a lot about how they should live their lives.

Many of them felt that they would spend more precious time with their loved ones. They learned there was so much more to life than their physical bodies and their material possessions. They felt that if they lived their lives full of spiritual virtues and quality human values, this better way of living would allow them to die with dignity, grace, and fearlessness. They all decided to use their new lease on life to live a more spiritual existence.

When we as living human beings recognize that we are all part of Oneness with the Divine Energy Source or God, we find the true purpose of living. Fortunately, we do not have to die to learn this. We can understand in this life that we are all part of one great cosmic story. We then no longer look at ourselves as individuals stuck in a mortal body that withers away to ashes in the end. We can see our life as a spiritual playground in which we use tools such as self-reflection, meditation, and prayer to practice spiritual lessons and spiritual virtues of the Universe, thereby preparing us through faith and hope for a death that is a birth into new life. These spiritual tools also include intention, the Law of Attraction, development of intuition, recognizing spiritual synchronicity, spiritual balance, development of higher consciousness, removal of self-doubt, and a life in which we constantly search our souls for the most righteous path we are capable of living. By proceeding in this way, we spread love to our family, friends, and the Universe, and we learn to give to all of them and expect little in return, because giving is always better than taking. If we are profoundly grateful for what we have, we will need to take truly little.

In the end, we must 'let go and let God.' By learning about our eventual transformation (death), we have an opportunity to learn an all-embracing sanctity of life. Embrace your transformation from this life to the next as a normal progression of living. When we accept our inevitable fate and regard it as God's loving plan, we will live our lives full of faith and hope, and our primary state of being will be a halcyon life.

Spiritual Awakening

A spiritual awakening is an epiphany or "Aha" moment in time. The spiritual awakening links your soul to pure consciousness, tying you to spiritual reality instead of an ego mind. In that moment, you feel the Divine Universe and the Oneness of all things, alive and dead. It is at this time that you know you are not your physical body. True reality goes beyond your five physical senses of sight, sound, smell, taste, and touch, and resides in your purest of selves where past, present, and future all meet to create celestial enlightenment that transcends life and death itself.

This is the greatest awareness you will ever experience. At this moment, you no longer question the purpose of life or whether or not there is a God. You now know in your heart that your purpose in life is to begin, or continue, your personal spiritual journey every day. You know, without hesitation, that there is a life after this one that is more purposeful and beautiful, where the physical body and world has been released to your Spirit, which enters the highest level of consciousness.

When we accept that our worldly death is simply a transformation to new life, we begin to live differently. All human beings are to be resurrected to new life, and all human beings will reach the Kingdom of Heaven. Death is a replenishment of life's energy into a more powerful Afterlife force of Supreme Energy and revitalization. By understanding the life-death-life continuum, we learn that everlasting life is our destiny.

Look around at our world right now and see the life-death continuum. Seeds of flowers sprout again, and we call them perennials. Most of the cells in our body die and are reborn. For instance, when we slough off our microscopic epidermal skin cells every four-to-six weeks, new skin cells replace them just as quickly as they leave. Did you know that there is a mature jellyfish called *Turritopsis dohrnii* that can revert back to a tiny early embryonic group of cells (sometimes referred to as the *cyst stage*) when it faces the threat of death? Afterward, the jellyfish grows back into its mature form. In this way, *Turritopsis dohrnii* is part of a life-death-life continuum.

Could this jellyfish live forever? Probably, just until someone in the animal kingdom eats him (Matsumoto et al.)

The circle of life is all around us. As elderly people perish, new babies are born. Our species prevails, potentially in perpetuity. The signs of the world tell us that life goes on forever. The first law of thermodynamics (conservation) states, "Energy is always conserved; it cannot be created or destroyed." When we go to sleep at night, we give our bodies time to replenish and revitalize energy lost during the day. In compliance with the first law of thermodynamics, energy lost one day changes into a higher energy the next day. Life's energy transforms to energetic life after death. When our physical bodies perish, the energy in our bodies is converted from physical form to a higher consciousness of energy in the Afterlife. Souls have spiritual energy that is never lost. Live your life with the understanding that your true self will never die and that true reality is everlasting life.

While you are living, replace the word "death" with the word "transformation" or "Crossover." Live your life unafraid of transformation. In time, your transformation (death) will be thought of as a crossroad into a better life. You can anticipate the transformation will fill you with love, beauty, Universal understanding, freedom, and happiness.

Live with Hope and Expectation

Now that you know something about what your future will look like, live without fear, self-doubt, anger, frustration, resentment, apathy, depression, or anxiety. In the Afterlife, you will find true love, will have greater freedom, and you will have Universal Knowledge/Universal Wisdom. You will experience the spiritual virtues of humility, honesty, integrity, peace, and joy. Your Spiritual Senses will include increased awareness, intuition, insight, creativity, and imagination. Your life starts slowly but builds to a wonderful crescendo of transformation into higher consciousness and enlightenment, known as the Afterlife.

Start to live now in a way that is similar to living in the Afterlife. Live each day feeling free and creative and in love with people and the nature of the Universe. Celebrate your life as having no limits or obstacles. Do not focus on despair and divisiveness. Know that there is nothing that can hold you back or bring you down. Go out and find or create the job you want. Find someone with similar spiritual beliefs to fall in love with and spend your time with. Be in love as much as possible. Learn to meditate and find spiritual synchronicities in your life (more on this later). Develop your ability to predict what will happen before it happens (intuition). Develop this intuition by believing your gut feelings are reliable. Trust yourself totally because you are completely honest with yourself and all those around you. Visualize the life you want, so you can easily create your own personal spiritual journey. Smile and be kind. Develop the spiritual virtues of life prior to your actual transformation. There are no limits to how extraordinary your spiritual awakening and implementation can be. Create a life for yourself that is restorative and fulfilling. It is through gaining a healthy perspective on death that we learn how to live a happier life.

Our imagination allows us to think from the end and work backwards. If we want to save $5000 in six months, we must use our imagination to visualize and feel the luxury of the money already in our possession. We see the end result before we even get started. This follows the Law of Attraction. Our intention is to accumulate $5000 in six months, so our imagination allows us to connect to Universal Spiritual Knowledge/Wisdom to make our money goal a reality.

In the same way, we can imagine our own death or life's ending and work backwards to achieve life's spiritual fulfillment while we are still alive. When you envision your own demise, you begin to realize the many things you would like to do and accomplish prior to your death. If you can imagine yourself about to die very soon or imagine yourself already dead, you can learn many things about your present life and learn very quickly about who you really are. Your authentic self will become easy to find. Your life's priorities and goals will rapidly become clear. You will quickly and efficiently connect with your spiritual self and will feel enlightened. Your purpose for living will become evident.

Exercise of Reliving Your Life

Of utmost importance to all of you reading this book is that you have a similar opportunity in your current mortal body to experience the living of your early life events. Using your mindful imagination, you can create a more metaphysical or spiritual life moving forward.

Lie down and get comfortable and close your eyes. Meditation at this time would be optimal, but if you do not know how to meditate (which you will before you finish this book), then just lie on your back and relax your body one hundred percent while closing your eyes. Now, imagine you are lying in an open coffin. Realize that you are dead. If you want, you can imagine how you died; that is, know the cause of your death. Now use your imagination to its fullest extent to see the main events of your life. You can start from the latest events and work your way back to the day you were born. If you prefer, you can start at your birth and work forward in time to your recent death. Whichever one you choose, remember you must visualize each event or experience you had while on Earth. Take your time with each event. Do not rush through your life's events.

Starting at birth, see yourself coming out of the womb. See the doctors and nurses suction the mucus from your lungs. See them get each of your Apgar scores as their faces show you're going to be a healthy or an unhealthy baby. See which family members are present in the hospital room or place where you were born.

Move forward to your childhood. What are your earliest memories? Think of these early memories and events. When did you first start to like or dislike things? What upset you, and what made you incredibly happy? Do you remember significant interactions with your siblings?

Move forward again on your life's timetable. Think about your school experiences. In your mind's eye, see one or two significant life-changing events in school. Think about and experience one or two wonderful friends. Make sure you clearly visualize all these experiences. What are your religious and spiritual beliefs? What are your feelings and emotional reactions to church or synagogue? Have you learned to pray or talk to God? Do you pray because you like it, or were you doing it because you were told to do it? Think about the spiritual life lessons you are being taught. Did you make spiritual virtues and points of view part of your everyday decisions and experiences?

Think about your prior significant love relationships. Think about your marriage, or if you haven't married, think about the person you connected with most on a spiritual level. If you have children, think about the time of their birth(s). Now, instead of just thinking about these events, relive them in detail in your imagination. How do you feel when you think about these events? Which emotions are stirred up? Did you always treat your spouse or significant other in a Godly, passionate, caring way? Did you ever strike your kids? When you hit them, was it truly out of love?

See yourself working in some of your jobs during your lifetime. Are you working just to put food on the table and have shelter, or is your job truly a labor of love? How passionate are you about your work? Have you stayed in this job too long? Do you treat your customers or patients in the way you would like to be treated, applying the Golden Rule? Have you been able to "put the shoe on the other foot?" In other words, can you feel what it is like to exchange places with your customers, clients, or patients? Have you been totally honest during every one of your employments? Did you ever steal any money or things from your job site? If you did, I want you to slowly relive that event in your mind's eye right now.

Move on to a later point in your life, especially if you reached midlife. Are there any midlife crises you're experiencing? Have you divorced yet? Are you planning on getting a divorce soon? See your significant past conflicts with your partner or spouse. Where did your love go? Did you and your partner work hard on your relationship? Did you ever develop a spiritual bond with each other? Could you have been a better wife, husband, or partner? Can you visualize the arguments over finances, child-rearing, things to buy, where to live, or your spiritual relationship with God and each other? See your life in your second marriage, if you had one. Were the problems the same or different than in your first marriage? Was the divorce your idea, their idea, or was it mutual? How would your life be different if you and your partner had made your spiritual selves more important than your egos and material possessions?

Answer all the questions to the best of your ability. Later, you will be doing a similar exercise when I teach you how to meditate. Hopefully, as you answer these questions throughout this book, you'll want to begin to improve on actions you took earlier in your life. When you get further in this book, the value of this exercise will become much clearer, as your life choices will begin to greatly improve.

The next chapter (Chapter 2) on spiritual lessons and spiritual virtues will address love relationships, your connection with the Divine Energy Source or God, employment, relationships with parents and siblings, honesty, selflessness, kindness, humility, and peace of mind. A few transgressions will also be mentioned. All of this information will help to enhance your perspective on what has transpired in your life to date. The next chapter will make all your answers to the previous questions about your past understood in an original way. You will start to find better questions and more astute answers to what has happened in your past and will receive the knowledge and wisdom needed to live better in the future. Your feelings, questions, and answers may change as you examine your life and death in this book going forward. As you read the successive chapters in this book, ask yourself, "Had I applied the principles in this book to my previous relationships and practices, would I have had a happier and more successful life?" Your feelings and answers to the questions will continuously evolve as you keep reading.

Now that you know something about the Afterlife, where death has already occurred, let's use the next chapter to delve more into spiritual lessons and spiritual virtues that can be learned both before and after death.

Affirmation: "My death will be my birth into a wonderful new life."

Live Like You Are Dying

CHAPTER 2
Spiritual Lessons and Spiritual Virtues

In human history, we are going from knowledge to omniscience, from potence to omnipotence, from ethics and religion to righteousness. So, in my view, God comes at the end of this long process. This may not happen in our lifetimes or even in the lifetime of our species.

—Martin Seligman

More on the Afterlife

Here in my Afterlife, people die and experience Crossover to the next life. When you cross over after your life on Earth, you move to another level of being or existence. Not everyone on Earth who dies moves to the same plane of existence (we may sometimes refer to this as a plane instead of a level). In other words, there are many diverse levels of Afterlife when you leave your life on Earth.

The righteousness we show in our current life is of crucial importance because we are held accountable in our next life. In each life, our purpose is to grow spiritually so that successive lives will give us greater inner peace and joy as we evolve closer to a heavenly existence.

After your Earthly life, you pass to a level of existence that is appropriate for your specific spiritual accomplishments. This is why you may or may not return to your deceased parent or grandparent when you pass from Earth. They may be on a different level than you. The spiritual lessons and spiritual virtues they still need to learn may be different than yours.

What is an appropriate Afterlife level for you? If there are spiritual lessons and spiritual virtues that you did not learn while alive on Earth, then your new Afterlife level will be one in which you get another chance to learn those specific spiritual virtues and spiritual lessons. For instance, if you continued to be selfish and never learned to share with other people when you were on Earth, you will find yourself on a level where you will be given opportunities to accept and practice the spiritual virtue of selflessness. If you never learned to trust yourself or others while alive on Earth, you will be given many opportunities to be educated in the spiritual lesson of trust while on your new plane of existence. Certainly, if you never stopped lying, or you continued to believe that murder was acceptable, or you continued the act of blasphemy, you would not move directly to the Kingdom of Heaven upon your death. You would need to learn and believe in the Ten Commandments so that lying, murder, and blasphemy would become repugnant to you. You would have to totally eliminate these transgressions from your behavior to grow spiritually.

The more spiritual lessons you learn in your Afterlives on various planes, the closer you will get to reaching your pure soul. A person's pure soul resides within himself and God. When there are no additional spiritual lessons and spiritual virtues to learn, you have reached a perfect state of purity and bliss. Some call this Nirvana or heaven. Of course, when you reach this state, you and all other pure souls are One with God. Once you have completed all of life's lessons and fully practiced all spiritual virtues, there are no more lessons to learn and no more lifetimes to participate in. Usually, it takes many lifetimes to reach spiritual perfection and become One with God and live eternally in the Kingdom of Heaven. Right now, I am on a level where I am learning how to be selfless and giving to others. I am learning how to serve God and to serve other spiritual entities. It is a shame that I did not become less selfish while alive on Earth, because I could have evolved more quickly to an advanced spiritual level.

When I was alive as a person with physical form on Earth, I always believed in an Afterlife. If someone would ask me, "Michael, do you believe in life after death?" I would say, "Yes, I do." However, I realize now that I did not live my life as if there was really going to be an Afterlife. I lived my life like I had unlimited time before I would die. I always thought death was a long way off. In reality, death was just around the corner. So many of us live our lives like we have so much time to live before we die. When we are young, we live like we are invincible. Had I fully embraced the notion of Afterlife as my younger self, I would've been able to digest more of life's lessons.

How do you live your life when you know that death is coming soon? If we are dying, and it is happening much faster than our conscious mind realizes, then how should we live? You may stop worrying about whether your weight is perfect. You may stop caring if you go to the gym one day a week or six days a week. You may stop caring if you buy a new car or a used car. You may not be concerned with whether you have $10,000 or $100,000 in the bank. Your body or physical form will become less important. You will become less materialistic. Belongings and physical things such as houses, cars, and clothes will have less significance than before your actualization of death. Remember, you are in the process of dying; you are actually transforming. We all are. Whether we are five years old, forty-five years old, or ninety years old, we are dying. Sometimes five-year-olds don't live to see their 15th birthday, and many ninety-year-olds do not live to see their 100th birthday. Whatever our age, when we cross over to our new Afterlife, possessions will not have any importance to us.

How can we be happy if there is no big home to work for and acquire? How can we be happy without vacations, travel, fancy clothes, and lots of money? Do we need to give up all the material pleasures available to us? We do not! Wanting to create large sums of money and attain luxurious possessions while simultaneously making these material things less important to us is a paradox rather than a contradiction. This progression from emphasizing material gain to finding it less important is an evolution of spiritual development. The Universe offers you an abundance of material things, and you are entitled to acquire and achieve them. Looking at it spiritually, God provides the Universe with an abundance of all things so you can rightly attain all your worldly desires. Wanting material gain for enjoyment is a part of being prosperous on Earth and is not a transgression—as long as true spiritual virtues are not violated. We can live with kindness and love while being materially wealthy as long as kindness and love are greater priorities than the material gains we wish to achieve. In this way, huge amounts of money in the bank and fancy cars and clothes become less significant than emotional and spiritual fulfillment attained prior to our Afterlife transformation. Especially as we age, our desires for love of family and peace of mind, which is spiritual in nature, supersedes previously admired belongings that become almost useless to us in our advancing age. With death coming soon, we become very aware that we cannot take our possessions with us.

We learn not to *worship* physical belongings since they are not permanent and should not be treated as sacred, but we are not required to give them up completely. Let me be clear here; I am not saying that you should never buy a new home, or a new car, or save $100,000. At the same time, develop your spiritual self and realize that this is the most important part of who you are. This is the *real* you. This is your authentic self. Materialism is not who you are. Material things are simply things you hold temporarily; they are not divine in and of themselves. They are never permanent because they break, wear out, or leave you, either during your lifetime or at the time of your transformation (death). You are a spiritual entity hosting a human life; you are not a human life hosting a spiritual entity. The closer we get to dying, the more satisfied we are, knowing that leaving our physical bodies and possessions behind is very acceptable and an inevitable human maturation.

Be happy as you actualize your immortality. Most people think they will just die, and most people worry considerably about dying. The idea of death makes them extremely sad. We do not die—we *transform*, which is also known as a *Crossover*. The spiritual lesson to learn is that death is just an illusion, because we can never be terminated. We leave our physical bodies and become spiritual entities without physical form. Death is truly rebirth.

No one can be genuinely happy while living in a physical body. You can be extremely satisfied knowing that when you cross over, you can never become physically ill again. You need a brain, heart, lungs, kidney, liver, bones, and skin that all fail to become chronically ill or have pain. When you leave your body at the time of transformation to your new life, there is never any illness or discomfort. Furthermore, you will be spending a lot more time on the many planes of your Afterlife than you ever spent during your lifetime on Earth. Since these new planes are filled with rapture and glory, this concept of endless time (or no time) is extremely welcome. You will consist of a higher level of consciousness without a corporeal form for eternity.

There will be no limitation to how far you can run or walk anymore. You will never be extremely hot or cold. You will not need a jet to get from the East Coast to the West Coast. There will be no limitations of time and space in your Afterlife. There is none in mine.

At the level I am at in my Afterlife, there is much kindness, love, peace, and gratefulness. Other entities are always giving me wonderful surprises and gifts. This all seems to be refreshing and new. The irony is that these same emotions and acts of friendship and love were all present in my Earthly life. Why do they seem so different now? The difference is that there is no contrasting criticism, resentment, judgment, or greed. There is little to no anger or violence. These are some of the main differences between this plane of existence and the Earthly life I had experienced.

Now that I am "dead" (but of course, I am not), I see how an Earthly life should be lived. Here are some day-to-day spiritual lessons for you: Stop judging others and smile. If you do not have something nice to say, do not say it at all. Do unto others as you would have others do unto you—this, of course, is the Golden Rule. Be sweet, be kind, love your neighbor, and love yourself. Be humble, gracious, merciful, graceful, and forgiving. The time to do all of this is now. Do not wait until you pass to the next life. Learn life's spiritual lessons now. Live life's spiritual virtues and live with good values. There is no time like the present because your death is always sooner than you think.

It is really a matter of perspective and priorities. Your spiritual self, as well as God, should be more important than mortal things such as money, cars, jobs, hairstyles, and clothing. Being a spiritual person who treats others with respect and love should always supersede a win or physical accomplishment. In the spiritual world, physical form is of the least importance; the most important things are positive thoughts, wonderful emotions, and all levels of higher consciousness.

A sophisticated spiritual lesson is the activation of your higher consciousness. In the Afterlife, no matter what level you find yourself on, higher consciousness prevails. It is possible to activate your higher consciousness on Earth, especially through meditation (which will be discussed later), but it is easily found in the Afterlife. In the higher consciousness, your pure intentions are paramount for spiritual success. Higher consciousness is keen intuition that surpasses logical reasoning of the ego mind. The higher consciousness involves divine thoughts (pure intentions) that create divine outcomes. Sometimes we refer to these as miracles. Higher consciousness involves spiritual thought that is supernatural, intuitive, and imaginative and often encompasses magical insight into future reactions and events. Higher consciousness creates events or happenings that are angelic, seraphic, saintly, and celestial.

My current higher consciousness allows me to make wise decisions because I can tap the higher Universal Intelligence or Universal Wisdom that originates from divinity. It allows for all problem-solving. My higher consciousness is one of love and peace. My highest level of consciousness allows for unity with Spiritual Oneness and God. At the highest level of consciousness, all entities are One with each other and with the Divine Energy Source or God. At this point, I am beginning to triumph over all transgressions and negative thoughts. My righteous intentions and my pure soul are part of my higher consciousness and are in unity with God, my creator. Higher consciousness is a form of enlightenment. You may or may not have reached heaven when your higher consciousness is fully developed. Higher consciousness is limited on Earth due to the soul inhabiting a physical form. I have not reached heaven yet.

It is obvious now that I should have been elevating my higher consciousness as much as possible while I was alive on Earth. I knew about the higher consciousness and understood it intellectually as I read about it, but I never understood much about how to use it. I certainly didn't know it was one of my spiritual lessons. I guess because I could not see it, I was not certain how to find it and employ it. I was not totally sure it existed. Let us discover later in this book whether I can help you find your higher consciousness while you are still alive. Meditation, which we will discuss and utilize later, can prove helpful for experiencing higher consciousness. There is also a later chapter devoted just to the subject of higher consciousness.

Life is an ever-changing process on a path of growth, both physical and spiritual. There is never really a goal reached without another goal taking its place. Even death is not the final destination to a life lived. The only so-called endgame that comes close to destiny is the Kingdom of Heaven with God, and even that has no end. Live truly in the moment because it is the process of living one's passions that makes us excited and happy, not necessarily the goal reached.

As we move forward in this chapter, let's further discuss spiritual lessons that must be learned in order to grow spiritually. These include a discussion on love, balance, spiritual synchronicity, and Oneness in your life with the Spiritual Universe. You will learn about additional spiritual virtues that we all need to practice on a regular basis. In later chapters, you learn spiritual actualization through meditation, prayer, and your relationship to Divine Energy/God. We will review the importance of the Law of Attraction, self-esteem, and death's role in our spiritual journey. These are the tools we use to reach higher consciousness and to grow our spiritual lives. The spiritual tools learned are necessary for a glorified life now and are needed by all for a glorified life after death. In the last chapters, I will touch upon the role of Christianity and religion in my belief system, and we can finish with conclusions regarding our spiritual life.

We never stop learning the spiritual virtues and spiritual lessons that we lack, both in this life and in our succeeding life or lives. It is only when we totally learn the spiritual lessons of the Divine Universe that we live with the Divine Energy Source or God in the Kingdom of Heaven for all eternity. Spiritual lessons sometimes incorporate the spiritual virtues and moral values that I will discuss and list below. Spiritual lessons also include eliminating avoidable transgressions, which are also stated going forward. Spiritual lessons and spiritual virtues are useless unless put into practice every day of your life.

Spiritual Lessons and Spiritual Virtues for this Life and the Afterlife

Honesty

There is an insightful adage that says, "Every lie is two lies, the lie we tell others and the lie we tell ourselves to justify it." Sometimes it takes courage to admit the truth to ourselves and others. It takes truthfulness to trust ourselves and to have others trust us. Honesty, truth, and trust are the cornerstones of integrity. With the spiritual virtues of truth, honesty, trust, and integrity, we will succeed in our undertakings because people and the Divine Universe will want us to do well. Divine Energy and Universal abundance will be our reward for practicing pure, virtuous behaviors.

I used to teach my children that it was okay to tell a white lie if it prevented another person from getting their feelings hurt. When my mom was 70 years old and still telling people she was 21, I was tired of hearing that white lie every year. It was then that I decided that maybe even white lies should not be appreciated.

Forgiveness

When we forgive others, we do not only make them feel better, but it removes our own inner anger and unhappiness. Forgiveness is Godlike behavior. When someone feels they have been wronged or hurt by another person, they feel the emotions of vengeance and resentment, and sometimes hatred. When these negative emotions fester chronically over time, only forgiveness will remedy these sickening feelings. The person who forgives may experience less anxiety, improve their self-esteem, and sleep better.

When I was 18 years old, attending college, and living at home, I came home one afternoon to find my father beating my mother. Over the years, my father had often physically abused my mother after intense arguments between the two of them. These arguments were often over money matters or my father's lack of participation in work that needed to be done around the house. I thought to myself, "Michael, you are not a small child anymore. Help her!" I pulled him off her, and he hit me—hard. We began a physical altercation. After getting in a solid punch to his jaw, I knew nothing good was going to come of this. I ran down the steps and out the side door, and he followed me. My dad was a police officer. As I ran toward my car, he pulled out his .38 Special handgun from its holster and screamed at me, "Stop, or I'll shoot!" I quickly jumped in my car and drove off. I soon moved out of my parents' house.

It took many years of feeling painful anger and resentment toward my father, but eventually I forgave him. I knew it made him incredibly happy when I did this. I was able to forgive him by reminding myself of all the good things my dad had done for me over the years. He had encouraged me to get a good education, took me to baseball games, taught me carpentry, played chess with me, and often showed me love the best he could. My father's transgressions had placed painful emotions deep inside me, and I didn't want the burden of experiencing those feelings any longer. By forgiving him, I could feel happier and free of hurt. The second reason I forgave him was because my mom always did, even though I realize that this was not a good reason for forgiveness. When I ultimately forgave him, I felt the world lifted off my shoulders.

Giving

Give to the Universe and the Universe will repay you tenfold. Giving and sharing with people, nature, and the Spiritual Universe will always return abundant blessings to you. If it doesn't happen in this lifetime, it will certainly return riches to you in the Afterlife. It takes a lot of maturity and much generosity to learn the spiritual lesson of giving and helping others. You do not have to give money unless you would like to. You can give your talent, expertise, and your time. You will find that giving will make you feel warm and fuzzy inside.

Gratitude

Gratefulness can be a difficult spiritual lesson to learn and acquire. When we are grateful for good health, knowledge/wisdom, loved ones, and our prosperity, we are looking at the glass as half full, and we stay free from sadness and unhappiness. When we continuously give thanks, we avoid negative thinking, bad behaviors, and unwanted emotions. Grateful people do not believe they alone have earned everything they have. They acknowledge that the Divine Universe is greatly responsible for their good fortune and achievements. Some people will call this good luck, and this is okay. I believe spiritually grateful people create their own good luck.

Gratefulness tends to harvest a garden of gifts. My partner, Kathy, loves playing and learning to play the guitar. I recently bought her a package of 10 guitar lessons because I thought she would enjoy that. Not only did she appreciate this gesture, but she became elated and deeply grateful! Her reaction set off a chain-reaction of emotion in me, and I can't wait to do more nice things for her. Her gratefulness will generate more gifts that she will receive. Your gratefulness to others will be returned to you by the Spiritual Universe.

When we are grateful to the Divine Energy Source or God for our health, talents, and all the gifts we have received, the Divine Universe rewards us with an abundance of additional prosperity. Taking inventory of the gifts we are grateful for creates optimism and success in all our endeavors. Try to give thanks daily, or even weekly, and your life will change dramatically.

Humility

Acting with Humility happens to be one of my favorite spiritual lessons. God, in his infinite wisdom, wants us to demonstrate humility. I like to look at humility as a special part of our personality. Righteous spiritual leaders like Mother Teresa, Gandhi, and Buddha all demonstrated immense humility. They were less concerned with their own aggrandizement and more concerned with helping those in need. Humility is the ultimate form of modesty. Humility makes us less important than humanity and respects others with more knowledge than ourselves.

People with humility are more likely to be good learners because they recognize their own weaknesses or lack of knowledge on a subject. They are open to learning because they welcome self-improvement. When humility is lacking, people develop obsessive pridefulness, self-centeredness, and narcissism. These are usually persons who think they are better than others. The world then finds them repulsive and immature. This can lead to poor self-esteem. A real estate developer who feels he must put his name on every one of his buildings shows no humility. That person is attempting to make himself or herself more important than the structure and its residents.

Peacefulness, Calmness, and Justice

Peacefulness and calmness are the hidden gems of the spiritual lessons. As we mature, peace of mind becomes paramount to our happiness. Inner peace and calm connect us with our gentle, loving soul. When we have inner peace, our positive and constructive thoughts set us up for rational decisions and success. Peace and calm indicate contentment and satisfaction with our lives. We cannot enjoy our lives if we are anxious and feel stressed. Worry and fear are the antitheses of peacefulness and calmness. Emotions of peacefulness and calmness create feelings of safety and tranquility.

Living peacefully means accepting that worldly needs and desires for possessions are managed, controlled, and balanced, and are no longer our main priority. Constant attempts to create huge amounts of monetary assets have been replaced with gratefulness for what we have already acquired as we delight in spiritual inner peace and calm.

The Bible states, "Those who make peace sow the seeds of justice by their peaceful acts" (*Common English Bible*. Jas. 3.18). We can attain justice through peaceful communication and negotiation. When societies consist of peaceful communities, collective peace may promulgate in countries, which leads to justice and peace among nations. Peace, calm, and justice are mainstays of spiritual righteousness. Walk with God, and you journey in peace and calmness.

Spread love to family, friends, neighbors, and the Universe

Spreading love daily is one of the most important spiritual lessons. Decide those to whom you will spread love. You may have to move outside your comfort zone. You can choose a family member, friend, acquaintance, or stranger. You may also choose animals (pets) or nature. The important point is to give more empathy, kindness, caring, and love than you normally would to the chosen subject(s). Note how you feel when you perform this activity. Take note of how this subject responds to you. Are they returning to you the feelings that you are spreading to them? Make your positive emotions towards them as genuine as possible.

You are part of a great family, and your entire family is part of humankind. Send love to your family and emit the message of love to the entire Spiritual Universe.

Love yourself

When you love yourself, it becomes easy to love others. People who are suffering from low self-esteem, anxiety, or depression find it difficult to be happy with the world. When you don't love yourself, most of your inner thoughts will be negative and destructive to yourself. These negative thoughts and emotions will be evident to family members, friends, acquaintances, and co-workers. It may become difficult for people to like you. If I am happy with myself, I can make others happy. If I can trust myself to be honest with myself, others will find me trustworthy. If I know I am a righteous person working on my spiritual growth, I will love myself.

There was a man who was a pathological liar. Whenever he was talking to others, he would make-up grandiose stories that could never be true. At one cocktail party, he told everyone that he had flown to space on a *SpaceX* rocket. He also told everyone that he was good friends with Elon Musk, the founder of *SpaceX*. Of course, we all knew this was not true. This man's exaggerations and lies were created to make himself seem important. If he loved himself and had high self-esteem, he would not have had to make up tall tales. This leads us to the next spiritual lesson: removing self-doubt.

Work to remove self-doubt

Self-doubt and lack of self-love are beliefs accompanied by emotions that are interconnected. Learning how to remove self-doubt and generate self-love are both lessons necessary to spiritual growth. People who have self-doubt usually have poor self-esteem. Low self-esteem goes hand-in-hand with a lack of confidence. When we lack self-confidence, it is difficult to be successful. Lack of confidence occurs when people have fears, usually a fear of failure. When people are afraid to fail, they may not even try things. When we are timid, limited action results in little to no accomplishment.

When I was working in plastic surgery, a lady came into the office for a rhinoplasty consultation. Rhinoplasty is a nasal surgery to fix or repair deformities of the nose. She told me, "I cannot find work because my nose is too big. I need you to make my nose as thin and as small as possible." From the patient history, I learned she admitted to seven prior nasal surgeries. Upon examination of the patient's nose, I could see several small scars and several irregularities of tissue contour. Her nose was as thin as a pencil, and the nostril openings were minuscule. It was already difficult for her to breathe. I told the patient that her nose was already too small for her facial features from an excess of prior nasal surgeries. The patient then told me, "Please just remove my entire nose!"

Obviously, this patient had unrealistic expectations and therefore was not an eligible surgical candidate. I diagnosed her with body dysmorphic disorder. Body dysmorphic disorder is a mental condition in which the patient experiences excess focus, anxiety, and shame over a perceived body part. The patient will often see the body part as more distorted than it actually is. The patient may believe that this body part is destroying their life. This patient was suffering from low self-esteem, was anxious, and lacked self-confidence. She had become greatly fearful of how people saw her. For this woman to be cured of her body dysmorphic disorder, she will need intensive psychological therapy over time. She will need help re-establishing her positive self-esteem and eliminating feelings of self-doubt. Some concepts for treating self-doubt include building self-confidence, learning to love oneself, attention to one's own abilities, learning to believe you were created in God's image, and much more. In a later chapter, I will discuss treating self-doubt in more detail.

Work on spiritual growth every day

When you wake up in the morning, remind yourself that you are a spiritual entity living in a physical body. Affirm to yourself that you will grow spiritually today by practicing spiritual virtues and spiritual lessons. Remind yourself to be kind all day and choose right over wrong.

Prioritize spiritual growth over materialistic accumulation. "You cannot take it with you" is the time-tested cliché. All of our possessions are borrowed. Everything we think we own will eventually leave our possession. Nothing stays with us forever, not even taxes. You can't even stay dead because you will be reborn. Strive to be the most righteous person you are capable of being. Look at the list of righteous words at the end of this chapter under "Practice the spiritual virtues of" and "Live with the highest moral values (standards)." How many of these virtues and values are you capable of expressing today and tomorrow?

Strive to be the most spiritually righteous person you are capable of being

Becoming spiritually righteous is a primary spiritual lesson. When I read the word righteous, I see in it the word *right*. It reminds me that I must do the *right* thing to act *right*eously. Most people know the difference between right and wrong; children generally learn the difference between right and wrong at an early age. We get into trouble when we don't choose the right actions or path. God gave us free will. People who choose a non-righteous path may do so out of greed (such as for monetary gain) or for power. A person who lies about his accomplishments at work to attain a promotion acts in an unrighteous, greedy manner so that he can have the job he wants (but doesn't deserve). Later, when the company finds out that he is a fraud, he may be fired from his job.

Being righteous means having good moral values. Moral values also help us distinguish right from wrong. When a person has good values such as kindness, respect for man, love of the Divine Energy Source or God, and honesty, he builds a personality of pristine morals that will guide all his life's behaviors. Through cooperation with others, helping others, expressing gratefulness, practicing patience, being creative, and continuing to learn, he strengthens his moral compass and approaches all endeavors with integrity. Righteousness and morality lead to cooperation among governments, societies, countries, and the Universe. Good moral values avoid chaos and anarchy among all peoples and nations.

Ethics are moral principles that guide a person's actions or archetypical behaviors. Ethics is the study of concepts of moral good versus moral evil and right versus wrong. When we choose righteousness and spiritual virtues over transgressions (or moral evil), we create moral goodness, and our actions are perceived as ethical. Ethics imply standards that suggest the following behaviors are morally wrong: fraud, violence, rape, stealing, slander, and murder. When we are spiritually righteous, we have a highly tuned moral compass and live with supreme ethical behaviors such as kindness, respect, honesty, responsibility, integrity, and trustworthiness. These latter qualities are what we all should all strive for.

Create patience and balance in your life

Go through life calmly and demonstrate patience and restraint. Keep balance in your life by keeping all likes and dislikes in perspective. Your ambitions should never become extreme fascinations. Have priorities, but do not obsess over them to the exclusion of everything else.

Get treatment for anxiety, depression, and other mental illnesses

To live healthily and perform well, we need clarity of mind. Our thoughts must be free from negative thinking, which—when extreme—can become mental illness. When we lose reality and live with phobias, fears, and delusions, we become unhappy and ineffective at coping with life's challenges and adversities. Please get professional help for all mental illnesses.

Live by the Golden rule

Do unto others as you would have others do unto you. Learn how to put yourself in the other person's shoes. Only when you live another person's life will you truly know what they feel and who they are, so do not pass judgment on others. When you see a homeless person on the corner, disheveled and asking for money, remember that if it weren't for Divine Energy or God, you could be that person.

Use affirmations, meditation, and prayer; create positive thinking by eliminating all negative thoughts

Meditation and prayer will enhance your spiritual growth. These will bring you closer to the metaphysical, cosmic, and spiritual worlds and connect you with God. Your health and happiness will improve immensely. Use creative affirmations to keep you on your spiritual path. One affirmation I love and use is, "I feel spiritually empowered and will make this a glorious day."

Use the Law of Attraction in spiritual ways to benefit yourself and others

Remember that you are as happy as you allow yourself to be. Be happy! Your positive thoughts will bring you happiness, and your spiritual journey will become easy. Making the Law of Attraction a spiritual law in your life is an essential spiritual lesson. The Spiritual Law of Attraction says, "Spiritually virtuous thoughts will create exuberant real-life experiences." In this way, the Universe will not be the only deciding factor in your fate or destiny. You will play an active role in bringing about all your wishes and desired circumstances. Reverent thoughts and intentions breed honorable outcomes instead of hedonistic experiences.

Avoid alcoholism and drug addiction

This, too, is a spiritual lesson. Alcoholism and drug addiction disconnect us from our authentic righteous selves and destroy our relationships with people and the Divine Energy Source or God. Use God to help you conquer your alcohol or drug addiction. Seek professional guidance to achieve sobriety.

Oneness with the Universe

Your spiritual lesson is to develop an awareness of your relationship with all living things, nature, the solar system, God, and the Afterlife. When we become One with all the Universe, our wisdom and our spiritual growth transcend commonplace mortal existence. Genuine joy then permeates our total spiritual being.

Spiritual Synchronicity

The Universe is giving us simultaneous events as signs and symbols to guide us on a successful path that has a purpose in our lives. This is known as synchronicity. Learn to see how repetitive clues and symbols are directing you to find meaning and solutions regarding imminent concerns. Universal Energy and Universal Wisdom are constantly finding solutions to fulfill our needs. We must be open-minded to the answers given in synchronicity by the Universe. When Divine Energy or God helps plant these symbols or signs to empower us, we call this a *spiritual synchronicity*. We will focus on how to recognize and utilize our personal synchronicities in another chapter of this book.

Build a strong relationship with the Divine Energy Source or God

Improve your relationship with God by speaking with Him or praying to Him. Read spiritual books and consider reading your religious texts or Bible. Develop the Spiritual Senses of awareness, creativity, intuition, insight, and imagination. Live the Ten Commandments and practice the spiritual virtues that are the Word of God. Follow God's guidance throughout your day and throughout your life. When you have done everything in your power to solve your problem(s) without results, let go and let God. It is now time for Him to help you.

Live like you are dying—because you are

This spiritual lesson is one of the most challenging because most of us live by clinging to life. We do not want to let go of life, so we avoid thinking of our death. Why not use your death to live a fuller life today? Wouldn't you do this if you knew you had two years to live? Study your own death to learn how to live more spiritually now.

Become conscious that your Earthly existence is only a speck of time on the timeline of your soul's eternal destiny. Learn to smile at death because it is your passageway to life everlasting. Do not fear death because it is not real. You are always reborn. Your physical form will not stay with you because it is only a shell for your true self, which is authentic and spiritual. Your spiritual self or soul will thrive forever after your mortal death in this world.

Know that someday soon, you will enter the Kingdom of Heaven. This is a grand event. You will enter the Kingdom of Heaven when all of the above spiritual lessons have been learned.

Practice the spiritual virtues of:

love honesty charity (generosity) giving gratefulness faith temperance forgiveness modesty patience prudence fortitude (perseverance) justice kindness humility hope peace calmness mindfulness (reflection and gentleness) joy.

Live with the highest moral values (standards) such as:

honesty compassion respect selflessness integrity empathy kindness cooperation courage loyalty fairness hard work acceptance altruism self-control responsibility caring open-mindedness friendship knowledge leadership optimism compromise trust.

Personality traits to avoid:

pridefulness greed envy lust gluttony jealousy hatred violence blasphemy stealing killing selfishness lack of remorse cruelty manipulation dishonesty narcissism sadism control issues racism bigotry meanness judgmental pessimistic egocentric neuroticism needing to be right stub-born manipulative vindictive aggressive passive-aggressive predatory unforgiving blameful sarcastic undermining.

Find the **Ten Commandments** listed below. It is not necessary to memorize them. Know them and incorporate them into your life. Notice how most of these commandments are as applicable today as they were over two thousand years ago. I urge you to particularly honor numbers five, six, eight, and nine. My reasons for giving unequal weight to each commandment is beyond the scope of this book, but I encourage you to evaluate the importance of each commandment in your personal life.

1. You shall have no other gods before me.
2. You shall not make idols.
3. You shall not take the name of the Lord your God in vain.
4. Remember the Sabbath day, to keep it holy.
5. Honor your father and your mother.
6. You shall not murder.
7. You shall not commit adultery.
8. You shall not steal.
9. You shall not bear false witness against your neighbor.
10. You shall not covet.

Now that you are at the end of this chapter, please think back to the questions I asked you to ask yourself in Chapter 1. Think of your answers, and contemplate whether the information in this chapter has affected any of your answers. Are you starting to see how your thoughts, attitudes, and Spirit life may affect the way you live in the future? Will you make the same decisions and practice your old ways of living? No difference yet? No problem. There are still many chapters to come that may change your mind and change the way you view the world so that you may live a better life going forward. Please keep an open mind.

Affirmation: "Today, I will spread love, kindness, and compassion to the Universe."

CHAPTER 3
The Law of Attraction and the Spiritual Law of Attraction

The person who sends out positive thoughts activates the world around him positively and draws back to himself positive results.

—Norman Vincent Peale

My Afterlife and the Law of Attraction

I am very much hoping to see my Grandma Rose in this Afterlife. In my previous life on Earth, she was one of my absolute favorite family members. As a child growing up, I always felt she loved my siblings and me so very much. She was warm, loving, and fun. She was always willing to play games with us. She loved card games, and I remember we often played pinochle with her. Grandma was a devout Italian Roman Catholic. She used her rosary beads every day, went to church every Sunday, and often went to church during the week as well. She was a member of the Rosary Society at her church and attended weekday meetings.

Grandma Rose was a stout old lady standing about 4'10" tall and had a square-shaped physique. She often smelled of a strong, fruity perfume right for her age. I remember Grandma would sneak me a quarter and say, "Make sure you do not tell Grandpa," as she gave a fleeting smile from the corner of her mouth. Everything about her was holy and special, and I loved her with every ounce of my being.

I decided to initiate an affirmation with the hope of bringing her to me. Every day I would meditate, tap my higher consciousness, and begin the repetitive intention (enhanced thought), "Grandma, I miss you ever since your death. I died but have been born again, and I am trying to find you. If you are able, please join up with me." While I was sending this message to the Universe, I would visualize my Grandma Rose in my state of higher consciousness. Her image was rendered in high contrast and with flawless clarity. It was like ultra-high resolution versus standard quality. I had never been able to form such clear pictures in my mind's imagination while on Earth. While I was visualizing her image, I allowed myself to feel the childhood love and devotion I always experienced when I was with her on Earth.

After many repetitive intentions of my affirmation made at different times, I knew Grandma Rose was about to come to me. I could smell her sweet perfume, feel her unconditional love, and hear the distinct voice only she could possess. She appeared as I knew her and not as an indistinct physical form like so many of the angels and souls appearing here. She looked exactly as I remembered her from about age seventy-five to age ninety-four. She had on her archetypal pink knee-length grandma dress with a little lace at the collar and décolleté. The dress was tight on her robust body, and her rosary beads hung too low. She still had her full-bodied white hair with a blue tint and appeared just like she always looked. It was Grandma Rose in all her splendor.

As my would-be-heart seemed to rocket from where the center of my chest would be on Earth (as I don't really have a physical body here in my Afterlife), I screamed, "Grandma, it is you! I am so happy to see you." I pushed my body towards her for a nostalgic hug when her body blended with mine in an exemplar wave of movement I had never experienced before. The well-known feeling of her genuine concern and love for me enveloped my being. I immediately asked, "Where is Grandpa?" She became jubilant and replied, "Grandpa is in the Kingdom of Heaven. He has been saved." My face lit up, and I cheered, "Oh my God. That is fantastic!" I felt a small tear run down my right cheek.

Then, I asked Grandma if I could see Grandpa, but she said, "souls in the Kingdom of Heaven do not leave, and we cannot visit with them." "This I did not know," I thought to myself. Then I asked her, "Will you be going to the Kingdom of Heaven soon?" She responded, "I am almost there. I have learned and lived almost all the spiritual lessons now. It will soon be my time to go." Once again, a small smirk formed at the corner of her mouth. I smiled and agreed with her that it had to be soon. She was always such a beautiful, pious person, and I was amazed that she was still here and not already in the Kingdom of Heaven. Grandma was the most holy and faithful disciple of Jesus I had ever known.

Grandma and I then reflected over our past lives. We discussed the game of pinochle and all the quarters she had given me over so many years. I had to ask her, "Grandma, how come you always told me not to tell Grandpa when you handed me the quarter?" She replied, "Grandpa was a good man, but he was always worried that I wasn't careful with his money." I said, "I see." There was then a long, complete silence between us, just like the silences we often experienced on Earth together. We both felt very content. Then Grandma surprised me when she asked, "Michael, would you like to see what I looked like as a young woman before I married Grandpa?" Startled and intrigued, but feeling she would really want to show me, I said, "Of course."

In a fraction of a second, a crystal-clear image of an eighteen-year-old Grandma Rose appeared. She was thin and looked taller than I ever could have imagined. Her hair was dark, long, and not that curly. Her facial features were wonderful, and she was radiant and beautiful. Her skin was white and soft without a wrinkle in sight. I smiled and laughed out loud and thanked her. I told her I never even thought about her as a young woman because, to me, she was always my Grandma Rose. She clairvoyantly said she knew that I thought of her as old and not young, and then she flashed her entire life's events before my eyes. It was a series of all the significant moments she had ever lived through. I experienced these moments with her from birth to age ninety-four, all in a fraction of time as we know it on Earth. This insight was miraculous. An electric elation ran through my entire being. I was fascinated beyond belief. In a childlike voice, while she slowly moved away, she whispered, "I will see you on the other side," and then she vanished.

The Law of Attraction

The Law of Attraction basically says that your energized thoughts attract people, objects, goals, and solutions into your life. Positive thinking about these things will manifest positive results, and negative thinking will have similar negative results (Lester 11). Every achievement or goal reached was initially begun by a person's single thought. In essence, we obtain something desired by first creating the thought of something we want. Now, people want many things and yet often never obtain them. So how exactly does this law work?

Your thoughts will have to be a repeated intention. When you passionately desire something aligned with your belief system, the thought may be referred to as an intention. To achieve almost certain results, the following should occur:

1. Repeated Intention
2. Affirmation or Auto-Suggestion
3. Visualization
4. A Feeling of Already Possessing the Desired Outcome
5. Emotion or Feelings
6. Perseverance
7. Meditation and Higher Consciousness
8. Prayer
9. Being Grateful
10. Belief in Divine Energy or God

The Law of Attraction is a concept that has probably been known for centuries or more, and many authors have written about it. In modern times, Meera Lester has written many books about The Law of Attraction. A well-known book, *The Secret*, reintroduced a similar theory of the Law of Attraction previously popularized by persons such as Madame Blavatsky and Norman Vincent Peale. The concept is that thinking certain things will make those things appear in one's life. *The Secret* also became a fairly well-known movie that highlighted the Law of Attraction.

Repeated Intention

The person with the desired goal should repeat their wishes often. This keeps the person focused on their objective(s). It allows their desire to remain at the forefront of their consciousness. This will also help prevent the goal or objective from being lost from memory. Furthermore, when we remind ourselves of things we want to accomplish, it is more likely that we will act. After all, thoughts without action will never result in achievements. Repeated intention also promulgates revisions of plans. As we are on a path to achieving our wishes, we sometimes find that it is best to modify the execution of plans for achievement to be made possible. This leads us to affirmation.

Affirmation or Auto-Suggestion

Affirmation is a prepared statement specifically declared to oneself that accurately depicts one's desire. It is like a mission statement that one chooses for himself or herself with words that will help him/her reach the desired goal. For example, if a person is seeking $10,000, his affirmation may become, "I wish to acquire $10,000 by December 31, 2022. This money will be given to me as a bonus by Smith Company for finding ten new clients in an eight-month period." Notice that the message of acquiring the money is specific in terms of amount, time allotted, and method of reaching the financial goal. This affirmation would then be repeated to oneself several times per day. In this way, the individual creates a believable and realistic clear path to achieving their money. There is daily repetition of their intention, and it is unlikely that the plan will be forgotten. Action is likely to occur because "creating more sales" is an unambiguous plan encouraging self-action.

Affirmation is comparable to auto-suggestion. In auto-suggestion, we repeatedly give ourselves positive messages to achieve our goals. Auto-suggestion is self-suggestion, which is similar to self-hypnosis. All of these terms are interconnected and can be used interchangeably. Instructing intentional messaging of the conscious mind also reaches the subconscious mind and sometimes a higher level of consciousness. With powerful thoughts in the forefront of our higher consciousness and subconscious mind, we strongly influence the world by use of all our senses. Our achievements are now easily realized.

When I was twenty-eight years old, I decided I must quit smoking so that I would have a healthy life. It was a time when most people were just becoming aware that smoking cigarettes would result in heart and lung disease. I had tried to quit smoking about five times but was having no results. Sometimes, I would quit for a couple of weeks or even months but then start smoking again. I was addicted to the nicotine in cigarettes and probably had a psychological addiction as well. One day, I was in the bookstore when I saw a book on self-hypnosis. I wondered if I could quit smoking with self-hypnosis and purchased the book. I read the book and learned that self- hypnosis was the use of self-suggestion. I then suggested to myself, "If I don't touch a cigarette, I won't smoke a cigarette." I would repeat this affirmation (self-suggestion or auto-suggestion) to myself several times a day and would put my hands in my pockets whenever I felt like smoking. It worked! I never smoked another cigarette, and after about six to nine months, I lost my desire to smoke cigarettes altogether.

When you give yourself an auto-suggestion, believe in what you are telling yourself and have faith in the outcome. Results will then follow. Starting with your intentions, it is helpful to infuse feelings and emotions to obtain the goal. It is a good idea to stop using phrases that begin with "*if* I reach my goal of $10,000" or "*if only I could* reach my goal of $10,000." Replace these words in the phrases with *when* and *I will,* respectively. In this way, you remove all doubt that the money will be obtained. Another good idea is to see and feel $10,000 cash in your hand right now. What is the texture of the bills? Imagine the feel of it in your hands. Are you already walking to the bank to make a deposit? See yourself walking to the bank with the money in hand. The phrase "See yourself" reminds me of the next tool to enhance your chances of success: Visualization.

Visualization

Visualization, just like it sounds, is when a person visualizes himself performing the action. This is necessary to achieve the goal. If our ambition is to own a new home, it is best to visualize oneself living in it. Seeing detailed images in our mind's eye of ourselves in the beautiful new bedroom suite or using the shiny stainless-steel appliances in a new home will empower us to make the purchase.

Try to imagine the images in as much detail as possible. This leads us to the idea of feeling already in possession of the desired outcome.

A Feeling of Already Possessing the Desired Outcome

To think we want something is a somewhat nebulous wish. On the other hand, if we believe fervently and confidently that the goal will be obtained, we begin to see ourselves already in possession of it. Start to talk to yourself and others about the process and the result of your accomplishment even though the objective has not been met yet. When I was about halfway through writing this book, I started telling everyone I was writing a book. I soon began to talk as though my book had already been finished. I knew that my words to others heard out loud would mean that there was no turning back. This book would have to be written. I began to see myself with a finished manuscript being submitted for publication. When you are already in possession of your future target, you most likely will actualize the results.

Emotion or Feelings

When we are passionate and excited about getting what we want, we are highly likely to pursue and achieve the desired conclusion. Victory is soon ours. Strong feelings make people and things seem highly animated and alive. When we feel elation at our thoughts of having riches or finally buying that new 3,000-square-foot home, our consciousness becomes fixated on making it ours. This leads us to a feeling of already being in possession of the outcome.

We have already learned that visualization and belief that you are already in possession of the goal or target may lead to success. It is the augmented feelings and emotions experienced during these two processes that increase the chances of a successful result. Realizing the purchase of a prom dress you always wanted will stir feelings of beauty, confidence, happiness, excitement, and femininity. With so many wonderful emotions felt prior to ownership, obtaining the prom dress becomes an easy reality.

Perseverance

To try to do something does not tell us anything about the strength of the attempt. If we persevere, the word implies that we will be relentless in our efforts until victory is achieved. Many people who have been extremely successful in life had little intelligence and talent, but they possessed the quality of perseverance. Failure is a stumbling block but not an obstacle for those who persevere. Going the extra mile is sometimes the only thing missing to reach one's objectives. When we push ourselves to do more than we think we're capable of, we go the extra mile. If I am expected to work for my employer eight hours per day, but I sometimes work nine or ten to get additional projects accomplished at work, I go the extra mile. When my wife asks me to vacuum the living room while she's gone, but I take it upon myself to vacuum the entire house and empty the dishwasher, I have gone the extra mile. Hopefully, I am rewarded at work with more pay and at home with my wife's reciprocity.

Anytime our persistence is endless, our failures are turned into victories. Sometimes, persistence is as simple as just showing up. How many of us have been ready to throw in the towel and quit our jobs, but we forced ourselves to show up at work the next day anyway? In time, the job got better, and we were really glad we didn't quit. Sometimes all that is required for success and achievement is to just keep going.

Meditation and Higher Consciousness

Let's simplify meditation for those who are turned off by the practice or don't feel they understand it. In a nutshell, meditation is your greatest level of awareness and concentration. Although you can reach a high level of consciousness both with or without meditation, meditation allows us to reach that higher level of consciousness more quickly and easily. Meditation is a freeing-up or open-mindedness of thoughts. When we meditate, we allow ourselves to have only positive thoughts and consciously remove all negative thinking. Successful meditation leads to calmness, creativity, peace, hope, and faith. Meditation allows us to release positive subconscious thinking, which enhances problem-solving and enables the discovery of meaningful solutions. Meditation brings us closer to our authentic selves and releases divine properties of our souls. We can emancipate Divine Energy and Enlightenment, which are two harbingers of our soul and our spiritual self, through meditation.

Inspiration, intuition, enthusiasm, and a relationship with Divine Energy or God are a few of the parts that make up our higher consciousness. When we introduce Divine Energy or God, along with higher consciousness, to the Law of Attraction, we are defining the Spiritual Law of Attraction. When Spirit is involved in our positive thinking process, we are utilizing the Spiritual Law of Attraction.

If we prefer not to use meditation, we can attain a higher consciousness by incorporating and developing the same personality traits of truth, faith, inspiration, creativity, intuition, synchronicity, self-confidence, and keen awareness by controlling our intentions and belief system (more of this in the chapter on Higher Consciousness). We can train our minds to think positively and aspire to these qualities of personality. Staying true to oneself and others is also necessary on each person's salient spiritual path. Meditation is just one helpful tool.

Prayer

Prayer also makes up The Spiritual Law of Attraction because faith is part of spiritual Divine Energy. Prayer, like meditation, enhances our ability to attract our goals and desires. Both in meditation and prayer, we can make a strong connection with Divine Energy within ourselves and in God's Universe. These Spiritual Energies give us the best chance of attaining our goals. If we stay focused and aware, we create a higher consciousness during prayer, which increases the likelihood of achieving our desired outcomes. By fervently tapping the faith residing in our souls, Divine Energy or God talks to us, and we listen faithfully to His instructions. When our spiritual growth is dynamic, the faith in the outcomes we seek becomes all-powerful, and all our dreams are actualized. With prayer, the Law of Attraction prevails as our positive prayers lead to prayers answered.

It is paramount that the things we meditate about and pray for are reverent and not frivolous or nefarious. Although the Law of Attraction leaves open the possibility that corrupt thoughts may deliver corrupt results, prayer may only entertain righteous requests. Prayer will be unheard by the Divine Universe when loathsome or maleficent wishes are requested.

Being Grateful

Be thankful for the gifts of life you already have and for the gifts or objectives you will soon receive. Appreciate the people who played even a small role in the path to your success. Feelings of gratitude will manifest in positive thoughts, which will be necessary on your route to victory. Thank Divine Energy or God for all the gifts and success given to you now and all gifts that will be given to you in the future.

Now, if this were just a personal growth book furnishing you a list of ideas to achieve your goals and ultimate success, we would incorporate ideas such as brainstorming, networking, marketing, advertising, creating long lists, self-messages on your refrigerator, and more. Instead, this chapter is focused on the ten spiritual tools needed to fully utilize the Law of Attraction so that Universal Good is achieved for your Glory—both here and in the Afterlife. In this way, the main focus of our discussion is the Spiritual Law of Attraction. This leads us to further discussion of the importance of our Spirit or relationship with God to attain all that we want, while always keeping the goodness of the Universe at the forefront of our intentions.

Belief in a Divine Energy Source or God

Your wishes are granted by the Universe when the Divine Energy Source or God gifts them to you. By embracing God's love, all our positive thoughts result in positive blessings from God.

The Law of Attraction says, "Your positive or negative thoughts will bring positive or negative experiences into your life." We can negate negative outcomes in our life experiences by utilizing the Word of God to acquire only positive experiences. Asking for things without engaging God may bring you what you want, but by linking desires with him, your desires are more likely to occur and will happen faster. For results to be inevitable, make purposeful and pious requests instead of unspiritual wishes. Wishing for a new suit may or may not get you a new suit, but wishing for Ukrainian children to be helped will more likely be gifted to you by the Divine Energy Source or God.

Whereas the Law of Attraction may incorporate a request for something that we want, such as material goods, a request to help others would be answered by the *Spiritual Law of Attraction.* Using the Law of Attraction to wish for worldly possessions for yourself is not a transgression. In fact, God encourages this. It is paradoxical that the Law of Attraction and the Spiritual Law of Attraction can both work in our Universe, and neither contradicts the other. It is not wrong to want possessions, but desiring ideas and devotions from your Spirit will produce more victorious outcomes. If I ask God to bring peace to the Middle East or use my intentions to bring food to starving children of the world, I am practicing a Spiritual Law of Attraction. The Spiritual universe or God will probably respond more favorably to these spiritual requests than my request for a new car. However, the car can certainly become mine, too.

Material possessions will never be as important in the Divine Universe as spiritual lessons learned. Any request you make regarding love, giving, charity, faith, hope, or peace is likely to be granted to you because of the Spiritual Law of Attraction. If you try to remove your fears or selfishness, you are most likely to receive these wishes when you allow Divine Energy or God to permeate your daily life's actions. When any of your thoughts are made in the pretext of goodness, the Divine Laws of the Universe are eager to give you what you want.

When you wish for your own spiritual growth and Divine Energy helps grant you this wish, the Spiritual Law of Attraction is at work. Because Spirit or Divine Energy of the Universe knows what we need more than we do, it is more likely we will receive requested wishes. When you not only ask for things you want, but also learn to give back (giving) to the Universe, Divine Wisdom that initiates the Spiritual Law of Attraction will fill you with a plethora of gifts. When you give to the Spiritual Universe, the Spiritual Universe gives you all the gifts you should have. Giving means receiving, so think less about what items you want and more about what your spiritual wishes should be. If you do this, your goodness will exemplify who you truly are, and you will be blessed with genuine riches and prosperity. Genuine riches that may come to you include good health for you and your children, as well as peace, joy, and happiness for long periods of time.

Things that you ask for may not be given to you until you cross over to your Afterlife or soon thereafter. Some of the things you desire will not be experienced in this lifetime. This may sound like the Law of Attraction doesn't work. Not at all. It just means that your thoughts and desires sometimes have to wait until the Afterlife to be actualized.

If you wish to strengthen your relationship with God, then use the Spiritual Law of Attraction to attract Him to you. Thoughts of God, which may or may not include prayer, will make your connection more powerful. As you entrust your life to God, your sentient being becomes filled with Divine Power, and wonderful things take place in your life.

Empowering God to you also makes your Afterlife lucid. You will hear God's message that you will re-unite with your loved ones. Your faith will solidify your understanding that pain and suffering are left in this life, and you will cross over into an Afterlife full of love and harmony. You will then be One with all the Universe (Universal Oneness). You will be free of your aging physical flesh and released from time and space limitations. You will have happiness, and all wishes will eventually be granted to you. On Earth, we cannot know with one-hundred percent scientific certainty that there is a God. By developing your spiritual faith in Him while practicing altruism to all persons now, God will arrive at your doorstep immediately and eternally upon your death.

Our passions should align with our spiritual belief systems and our requests, desires, and goals. Passions are telling us our heart's desire. When we decide what career to choose for ourselves, we should be passionate about the service it provides. Whoever makes career choices based on their passions tends to find a long-lasting, rewarding career. For myself, I was interested in learning about the human body and in helping ill people, so after much soul-searching and prayer, I became a physician assistant—a profession which I mostly enjoyed for the mainstay of 40 years. As they say, "Perform a job based on what you love in life, and it will never feel like you are working." When we are passionate about the things we desire, the Universe seems to grant them to us. Pick a career that you will respect and work in a way that God will admire. Pray to God that you will find and live your passion.

Imagination, creativity, insight, intuition, and intention are all part of the spiritual energy of the Universe. Of course, I believe this to be the Divine Energy source or God. Imagination and creativity allow us to see the end of our lives and work backwards. See yourself in your Afterlife, having crossed over from this world. Have all your hopes and dreams been answered? Were your desires and wishes achieved or given to you while on Earth? Did you always follow your heart's desire as well as your intuition? Were you always passionate about your work? How did you achieve your goals while alive? Did your thoughts and intentions in your higher spiritual consciousness become your life's experience? If the answer to some of these questions is "not really," it is not too late. You still have time (although you cannot be sure how much) to acquire all that you want. Now stop thinking about these questions as someone who has died, find the Spiritual Law of Attraction today, and begin to put it into action.

Realize now that life is infinite. When we lose our physical bodies, we still live on. Our soul is eternal. If your desires are righteous and reverent, the energy of infinity will richly reward you. God's love is not only part of this life but also for all eternity. God loves you now and after your Crossover to the Afterlife. His love grants all our pious requests from the abundance of the unlimited Universe. "Keep on asking, and you will receive what you ask for. Keep on seeking, and you will find. Keep on knocking, and the door will be open to you" (Matt. 7.7). All of this happens when you strengthen your relationship with the Universal Energy Source or God.

Affirmation: "Using the Spiritual Law of Attraction, I will conjure up righteous wishes to create worthy desired outcomes."

Live Like You Are Dying

CHAPTER 4
Meditation

There is no good or bad meditation - there is simply awareness or non-awareness. To begin with we get distracted a lot. Over time, we get distracted less. Be gentle with your approach, be patient with the mind, and be kind to yourself along the way.

—Andy Puddicombe

Meditation in My Afterlife

Two spirits and I decided we would meditate together. Their names are Matthew and Paul. In the Afterlife, I am known as Michelangelo. Since the three of us are all telepathic and clairvoyant, today we decided we would all simultaneously meditate on the same subject. We were having trouble producing the subject to meditate on when Matthew said, "Let's just have a fun day. Let's pick a sport that was the most fun for us when we were alive." Immediately, we all thought of golf. We decided to use our imaginations while meditating to play golf using only our higher consciousness.

We found ourselves at the Augusta National Golf Club in Augusta, Georgia. This is the course where the Masters Golf Tournament is played every year. For you non-golfers, it is golf's most beloved men's major golf championship of the four golf majors.

The three of us decided we would play from the "tips," which is the longest yardage on the course. We then decided to play hole number one, the sixth most challenging hole on the course, named "Tea Olive." It is a par 4, 445-yard hole with a difficult upslope and a fairway bunker on the right as well as a greenside bunker on the left. Just when we were about to tee off, Matthew had a great idea. We would make it a foursome by inviting Arnold Palmer to play with us! "Arnie," as he was known on Earth, passed away on September 25, 2016, but many of us knew he was still playing a lot of mindful, meditative golf in the Afterlife. We asked him if he would play golf with us, and he decided to join in. We had our foursome.

The four of us then proceeded to hit our drives. We all hit good tee shots, and our athletic juices began to flow through time and space. We were hopeful that the "golf gods" would be with us (lol). To make things interesting and fun, we decided to have the winner awarded $1.3 million (although there would be nowhere to use this money in the Afterlife). We only imagined this because all of us had fantasized about winning PGA Tour prize money when we were alive. Even Arnie had never won that much money for one tournament while on Earth. We all made par on the first hole.

We found ourselves at hole number three, called "Flowering Peach." This par 4, 350-yard hole is fascinating because you can either choose to lay up and leave a wedge to the green or try to drive the green off the tee. We all decided to go for it! We hadn't come here all the way from Earth to the Afterlife *just to lay up*. All of us hit the green in one shot, making our dream of reaching a par 4 with one swing of the club come true. When we arrived at the green, Paul sensed his higher consciousness beginning to wander. Thoughts of a recent prayer he made to God became a distraction to him and to all of us because of our keen sense of awareness during the meditative process. We all quickly stomped out Paul's thoughts of prayer. When we meditate, we must not permit thoughts that are not related to the chosen subject. Since we had decided to focus on "golf fun," the thoughts of prayer had to wait. For now, we eliminated thoughtful prayer. We all went on to make birdies on hole number 3. We were all elated.

We then moved via astral projection to hole number 6, called "Juniper," because we all adored this little hole. It was a par 3, 180-yard challenge because the green's surface could be very slick. We all hit extremely high shots that only a professional could hit, and they all hit and held the green very well. Paul and Arnie's shots had both released upon hitting the green, and they both made hole-in-ones (not likely at all on Earth), and Matthew and I made birdies. By God, this was fantastic!

We all decided that it was time to enter "Amen Corner," which consists of holes 11, 12, and 13, considered the most challenging three consecutive holes on the course. We all agreed to play hole number 11, "White Dogwood," a par 4, 520-yard beast of a hole. The tee shot would need to hug the right tree line. When Arnie hit his tee shot and his golf ball crashed into the right trees, he screamed, "Trees are our friends!" The golf ball listened and immediately ricocheted left and forward into the center of the fairway. At that point, we all agreed that any shot we mistakenly hit into the woods would bounce back into the fairway. This is something we all wished for while playing golf on Earth. We finished the hole with two eagles, a birdie, and one par. Arnie was in the lead.

We literally flew to hole 13, appropriately named "Azalea" for all the azalea flowers at Augusta National. It is the last hole of Amen Corner, and it is a Par 5, 510-yard right-to-left design. We all hit perfect right-to-left draws off the tee, which were hit about 345 yards and landed in the middle of the fairway. I don't think even Arnie could drive it 345 yards when he played on the Tour on Earth. While alive, the rest of us could only dream about hitting a golf ball this far. Paul and Matthew made par, Arnie made a birdie, and I made an eagle. I hadn't made an eagle in 10 years. Arnie was in the lead by one stroke over Paul.

We were having the time of our lives, but it was time to move on to the eighteenth hole. This hole is known as "Holly." It is a par 4, 465-yard uphill dogleg right, with a narrow chute of trees off the tee. The bunker in the left fairway always found many a tee shot. We all played nice left-to-right fades off the tee. Suddenly, Paul yelled, "My 8 iron is missing!" Then Matthew screamed, "I can't find my rangefinder!" We all laughed simultaneously. Even with our keen, meditation-enhanced senses of awareness and intuition, a golf club and a rangefinder were misplaced. We then used our meditative higher levels of consciousness to find and retrieve the misplaced belongings. With the lost belongings found, we were ready to finish our round of golf.

In the end, we all putted well and made three eagles, two aces, ten birdies, and nine pars between the four of us. We all shot rounds in the 60s, which were scores only Arnie had shot while alive. Paul ended up the winner, but he refused the $1.3 million with a wry smile, saying, "I certainly won't need it where I'm going." It had been a wonderful day of fun using our imaginations, creativity, intuition, and of course, our ability to meditate. We had created a spectacular round of golf that none of us—except maybe Arnie—were capable of producing on Earth. Sometimes it's so good to be alive, I mean dead, I mean alive, I mean dead...

Meditation

Meditation can be defined as using one's deep thinking to create a keen awareness and elevated level of concentration that is usually focused on one thought or thing while using one's higher consciousness. Meditation is usually done in silence while a person actively calms his being. It is often used for spiritual purposes or religious reasons but can also be used as a method of relaxation. Meditation brings to mind words such as deep thinking, concentration, contemplation, introspection, reflection, self-examination, pondering, and quiet time.

The words *meditation* and *meditating* may also conjure up mental pictures of men in robes sitting in cross-legged lotus positions, either barefoot or with sandals. One may think of men with long hair and beards looking somewhat disheveled. These are, of course, incorrect stereotypes of those who meditate. In reality, in today's world, folks who meditate are of both sexes and almost any age, come from all walks of life, dress in modern-day clothing, and can look like almost anyone.

Meditation may date back as far as 5000 BC. The practice itself has connections to Egypt, China, and India. Early Eastern meditation was associated with religions such as Buddhism, Hinduism, Jainism, and others. In the 1900s, meditation spread quickly as people became passionate about the activity when the Beatles and other celebrities were practicing Transcendental Meditation and making trips to India to learn its techniques. Transcendental Meditation is a specific form of meditation in which the subject uses a mantra (a repetition of words or sounds) while sitting or lying in a relaxed position. Maharishi Mahesh Yogi has been given credit for developing Transcendental Meditation in India in the 1950s (factsanddetails.com). The idea of this meditation is the avoidance of distracting thoughts, thereby creating higher consciousness and discovery of a spiritual experience.

Many scientific observers have found that meditation may decrease high blood pressure, improve breathing, reduce chronic pain, diminish anxiety, and treat depression. Supporters of meditation believe that in addition to improved health, they experience new levels of consciousness, greater happiness, more creativity, increased productivity, success, spiritual growth, out-of-body journeys, and enlightenment.

It is this author's belief that when people practice meditation, each person's experience is different and specific to themselves. I use meditation myself to find clearness of thought, peace, and spiritual guidance. I find that meditation strengthens my prayers to God and Jesus. Meditation can help us pleasantly escape *ego reality* and find more creative thoughts and solutions. Meditation initiates spiritual virtues and makes it easier to learn our spiritual lessons, thereby making us better human beings. Focus on material gain becomes less important to us as spiritual introspection makes us joyful. In meditation, we send kindness and love out into the Universe and enhance our relationship with Divine Energy or God. When we meditate, we find ourselves becoming more intuitive, insightful, and imaginative, which enables us to find success and prosperity in our relationships and in life's endeavors.

In my mind, there are three types of meditation. They are simple, moderate, and advanced meditation. All meditation requires quiet surroundings in the most comfortable position you are capable of. The exact position is unimportant. When you meditate, you can think to yourself, or you can be verbal and talk aloud. This is your choice. If your version of meditation is humming, or making sounds, or chanting instead of using words, this is fine as well. It is usually best for most people to close their eyes, but this is not a must.

Simple Meditation

Simple meditation involves thinking about one simple thought, such as your own breathing, or looking at a candle in your mind's eye. If you prefer to open your eyes and observe a real candle burning, this is okay, but I warn you that the surrounding visual environment may distract you. It is important that nothing distract you while you are meditating. You will find that unwanted thoughts unrelated to your breathing or the candle (or anything else you may have chosen to meditate on) will unexpectedly pop into your mind. Stop these thoughts immediately and return to the breathing, candle, item, or idea you are meditating on. Blocking extraneous thoughts from occupying your conscious mind will be exceedingly difficult at first. It is different for everyone, but it may take weeks or months to control unwanted thoughts. If you persist, you will be successful. This is the essence of simple meditation. The results it produces and the time it takes to produce these results will vary with each individual. People ask, how long should I meditate? I recommend starting with five minutes, one-to-two times per day, and working your way up to fifteen minutes, one-to-two times per day. Remember, your goal is to only think about your breathing or the burning candle. When you are experiencing an unrelated thought, then you are not meditating. Meditation is the ultimate form of mind control.

Intermediate Meditation

The next stage of meditation is the intermediate form of meditation. This is called *mindful meditation*. You should not try this form of meditation until you have mastered simple meditation because you will find it too difficult. Again, wear comfortable clothes and sit in a relaxed position in a quiet environment by yourself. It is preferable that you close your eyes, but this is not an absolute requirement. Group meditation is also an option. People can have group meditation, if they prefer, after they have some experience with solo meditation.

In intermediate meditation, you're going to do more than concentrate on your breathing or observe a burning candle. Intermediate meditation is linked with mindful meditation. Mindful meditation involves allowing your thoughts to originate without an impetus from your ego mind (inner voice). No matter the subject matter, refrain from stopping any thoughts that pop up without your intention. These are thoughts that come into your conscious mind, unprovoked by you. When you become aware of a new thought, just observe it. Do not try to direct or redirect the thought, stop the thought, or expound upon the thought. You should see yourself as an outside observer looking upon the thought(s) only. It should feel as though the thought or intention is not even created by your conscious mind. Your awareness of the thought or thoughts should be keen and definitive. Do nothing with it but observe it and see it clearly. This is the ultimate form of observation. You are now replacing typical awareness with enlightened awareness.

In intermediate meditation, your next unprovoked thought should replace the prior thought and may or may not be related to the same subject matter. Your mind must not force anything, acting only as a keen observer. From this intermediate meditation practice, many people find that the thoughts presenting themselves are important to them right now in their daily lives. Sometimes the meditator is not even aware that his mind was focused on these ideas or thoughts, and he didn't even know he cared about such things. At other times, the meditator will observe that the thoughts that surface may actually be solutions he was trying to find to current problems.

In this way, it becomes obvious that many of these thoughts and intentions originate from the meditator's subconscious mind.

Sometimes, unprovoked thoughts that appear to the meditator will be of a spiritual nature. They may present as thoughts and feelings that are kind, loving, and giving. If any evil thoughts occur while meditating, do not be too concerned, as they will be self-replaced by better thoughts before long. Later, when the meditation is over, you can reflect back on your virtuous and evil thoughts and explore them in your ego mind, if you wish.

Sometimes, in intermediate meditation, we may have thoughts about future events that may relate to almost anything. The human mind always has some level of doubt and anxiety about the future because the future is uncertain. As a means of protection and self-preservation, both the ego and the subconscious mind attempt to predict future events and solutions as a way of feeling safe. Some of these thoughts may come to pass in the future, and others will not. Just allow these thoughts to enter your mind, no matter how irrelevant or preposterous they may seem at the time. All spiritual entities have varying amounts of intuition and clairvoyance. In developing the spiritual side of yourself, you will become better at knowing things that will happen before they take place. Both your abilities of intuition and clairvoyance will become more developed. Your levels of keen awareness and ability to focus will be immensely enhanced.

Advanced Meditation

The third and most important type of meditation is advanced meditation. I recommend you don't attempt to perform this until you are comfortable with simple meditation and intermediate (mindful) meditation. The skills that you will develop in simple and intermediate meditation will allow you to be successful at advanced meditation. Trying to perform advanced meditation without the skills of the first two types of meditation will set you up for failure and most likely discourage you from ever enjoying the rewards of meditation.

There are many advanced meditation techniques available. In fact, there are an unlimited number of advanced meditation techniques available to all who partake in meditation. At some point, you may even create your own way to perform your advanced meditation. I would even encourage this when you feel ready.

The best techniques of advanced meditation open a window to your soul and your authentic self. These forms of meditation can give you good health, joy, and a stronger connection to yourself, God, and the Universe. These techniques may ultimately create wonderful emotions, superior thinking, a keen intuition, solutions to predicaments and problems, and much more. You may even decide to combine meditation with prayer. When meditating, if you combine your intentions, the Spiritual Laws of Attraction, and your purpose in life, it is very possible that you will achieve success in all areas of life that are most important to you. If love is your desire, you will find it. If finding a reason to live is your bailiwick, the answer will come to you. If financial gain is your priority, you will gain these riches. If good health is your main concern, you will become healthier. When you meditate, ask and you shall receive.

When performing advanced meditation, as with the other techniques, put yourself in a comfortable, relaxed position, lying on your back or sitting comfortably in a chair. Calm yourself, relax all your muscles, and start by meditating on your breathing. When you are ready, begin advanced meditation.

Advanced Meditation Technique 1:

Imagine yourself attempting to find a solution to a problem that you have been working on or a situation that you feel worried or fearful about. During this advanced technique, you will be focusing only on this one issue. If thoughts unrelated to this problem enter your mind, immediately stop the thought, and begin again on the problem at hand. Let your inner voice ask a question that the problem or undesirable situation creates. You must first have extreme clarity of what the problem or undesirable situation is. You must describe to yourself, in detail, the complexity of the issue. When your understanding of the events and issues that led up to the problem or strife is clear, then you are ready to let your higher consciousness find solutions. Imagine your mind is a clean chalkboard. Do nothing at this time except observe multiple answers appear on the chalkboard without any help from your conscious (ego) mind. These answers are coming from Universal Knowledge and not from you. Make sure you see at least five solutions before moving on. Now, permit yourself to creatively find solutions to the problem. See each solution in detail. Use all the creativity, intuitiveness, and insightfulness that your higher consciousness can conjure up. Remember not to think of anything else unrelated to your problem-solving. When you feel you have made progress and have some solutions, clear your mind again. Now, give thanks to the Universal Energy or God for having helped you find these answers.

Advanced Meditation Technique 2:

Choose any subject that you would like. For descriptive purposes of how to proceed in Exercise 2, I will choose the subject of health, but you may choose something else. Get into your typical relaxed position, calm your mind, note your breathing for a minute or two, and prepare to focus on the chosen topic. The important thing in this exercise is that we will pepper it with our spiritual connection.

To start, try to feel the presence of Divine Energy, or God. This will be individual to each person. Some people will want to see a bright light while they meditate. Others will have an idea of what God may look like. The important thing is that we use our heightened awareness, creativity, and insight to experience our connection with the Spirit. If you are Christian, you may want to connect with the Holy Spirit at this time. You may feel warmness and love or an empowered feeling of enlightenment or Universal Knowledge. You will know that you are not alone. You are going to experience this meditation with Divine Energy of some sort.

Now think about your current health. Some people feel extremely healthy, and others feel less healthy. You know where you fall in the health spectrum. What parts of your body are the weakest? Is it your liver or pancreas? Is it your small or large bowel? Do you have problems with arthritis of the joints or muscle and bone pain? Do you have any cancers in your body? Now focus on these weakest areas of your body. Try to imagine what they may look like. What is the problem with that organ? Does it have decreased blood flow? Is it loaded with inflammation or cancer cells? Now, ask the Divine Energy or God to look at these sickly organ systems with you. Ask God if he can empower you to repair these poorly functioning organ systems. Believe with all your heart that Divine Energy or God is with you and is willing to share Divine power to heal. Now, visualize your organ systems improving their functions. Try not to think about whether or not this is possible. Try not to be skeptical or negative in your thinking. Just visualize blood flow improving.

See toxic waste flowing away from these organ systems while healthy antibodies and lymphocytes infuse all of the diseased areas responsible for your illnesses. Do not allow any unrelated extraneous thoughts. Stay focused only on the topic of healing your body. Your meditation is becoming successful. You are visualizing improvement in the color and size of your organs as well as healthier blood and lymphatic flow everywhere you look. You can now feel the emotions of happiness and joy as you are certain that you are on the road to good health. You thank Divine Energy or God for having given you this power today to heal yourself. It is your own body that has destroyed illness and disease today. You now clear your mind and listen to your breathing, feel your relaxed muscles, and begin to slowly open your eyes. Your meditation has been a success, and you will be back again tomorrow to repeat this advanced meditation process.

Advanced Meditation Technique 3:

As usual, dress comfortably, relax your body completely in either a sitting or lying position, and be still with your eyes closed.

See yourself dead in your funeral casket. You are lifeless in the funeral parlor with your relatives and friends there to pay you their last respects. Observe your age at the time of death. Are you old, young, or your current age? Thank everyone for coming even though you are dead. Who is there, exactly? Who isn't there who you thought would be there? How did you die? Was it a short or prolonged illness? Contemplate and answer these questions without letting your mind wander to any other subject.

Now, while meditating, reflect back on your life, allowing the most momentous events to have the highest priority. Think of the early years of high school, college, relationships, marriage, and employment history. Did you live in a different part of the country or world? Did you have any serious illnesses? Were you religious or spiritual while alive? Did you ever save someone's life or kill someone? Did you share your life with someone? Did you ever own a car or a house? Did you acquire a lot of money or a modest amount of money in your lifetime? Were you materialistic or were you spiritual? Did you value your material possessions more than your acts of love, kindness, and spiritual growth? What were your family and friends like? Go into a little detail or a lot of detail. Hopefully, at later dates, you will perform the same meditation in increasing detail. Was there anything you would have done differently? Did you ever take your life or your relationships for granted? Were you loving and kind all the time? Did you find your purpose in life? Did you believe in an Afterlife? Was your life too long or too short? Did you do all the things you wanted to do? Was there something you wish you would have told someone while you were alive?

While performing advanced meditation, keep asking your own questions and keep hearing the answers come to you. When you feel saturated, and the exercise has become tiresome, stop your meditation. You should not strain your mind or allow this exercise to become stressful. You are not expected to ask and answer all the questions in one meditation sitting. You may ask some of the questions today and leave other questions for a future meditation day.

Lying comfortably, keep your mind clear for ten or twenty seconds with your body muscles relaxed. Do not move. Open your eyes. Think back on the meditation. Do you feel that you learned anything yet? How do you feel about your life? Think about how you feel about your spiritual life. How did it feel being very connected to Divine Energy or God? Answer these the best you can by using your usual *internal voice* or *ego consciousness*.

To summarize the advanced meditation technique, it is paramount that we concern ourselves with only one subject. We must stick with that subject throughout our entire meditation. Although we picked the subject of health in Advanced Meditation Technique 2, we could have picked any subject. What makes Advanced Meditation Technique 3 different is that we are performing it from the perspective of having died. Often when we imagine ourselves dead, we find an urgency to live the best life we can. We often feel that we have a second chance to live a more virtuous spiritual life. We learn that our physical possessions are not who we are and that they are fleeting. We realize that our physical bodies fail us, but our spiritual authenticity can never fail because it is truly who we are. We are a spirit and a soul with everlasting life. The purpose of this lifetime is to learn spiritual lessons that help us to grow Godlike on our path to reach the Kingdom of Heaven. It becomes important to us to practice acts of love and kindness and demonstrate integrity. Spiritual growth is a process and requires mental discipline. Meditation is the highest form of mental discipline. With continued meditation, we will feel as though we have shed our physical bodies. When we release ourselves from our physical shells, pain and suffering cease, and we bring good health to the Afterlife for eternity. One of life's spiritual lessons is to reach our spiritual higher consciousness, which becomes quick and easy with the tool of meditation.

Affirmation: "Through meditation, I will connect with my higher power, known as higher consciousness, to find my true purpose in life and death."

Live Like You Are Dying

CHAPTER 5
Balance and Spiritual Balance

When the material, psychological and spiritual dimensions are brought into balance, life becomes whole, and this union brings feelings of comfort and security.

—Deepak Chopra

Spiritual Balance in My Afterlife

I am sitting on a pink, gaseous form in my Afterlife. My legs are crossed in the lotus position, and I am comfortable and relaxed. I never had the flexibility to sit comfortably in this position when I lived on Earth, so I am really enjoying this capability. As I sit with a smile on my face, experiencing all positive intentions, I suddenly become aware of about one hundred similar spirits dispersed around me in geometric rows. We resemble fans at an Earthly sports stadium.

Just then, in walks an indistinct formless clown-faced spirit, juggling seven balls above where his head should be. The balls are equally spaced, and the clown's hazy body form is positioned for superb balance. Appearing to his right are two childlike gaseous spirits of the same size who also have unclear physical forms. They are on an Earthly dream-like playground seesaw. There is no need for their feet to push off the blue gaseous platform since the seesaw is parallel to it, and the seesaw is perfectly suspended and balanced. The children's feet dangle in space as they laugh out loud. Above them all is a tightrope walker who is moving across a free-floating high wire with perfect steadiness and impeccable balance.

This is a performance for the benefit of all the Afterlife spirits present. It is jovial and reminds me of an Earthly carnival or circus. However, there is a serious undertone of an important theme present. We, the spirits, are all viewing ideal balance. This is a demonstration of the physical form of perfect balance, which represents Spiritual Balance.

The juggler, the childlike spirits on the seesaw, and the tightrope artist all fade into ethereal gases. The one hundred spirits I am sitting with seem to vaporize before me; they are gone. My thoughts turn to Spiritual Balance, and I am slightly confused, as I am not certain what Spiritual Balance means. At that moment, two sparkling cerulean blue angels with halos appear in front of my being. They present me with judicious explanations of Spiritual Balance. They tell me that Spiritual Balance is a large portion of Universal Wisdom and Universal Energy. They alternate in expressing to me the following principles of Spiritual Balance: "Balance most often applies to our physical forms. Using exceptional physical form and balance, we can dance like a ballet dancer en pointe, swing a golf club like Tiger Woods, play guitar like Eric Clapton, pitch a baseball like Nolan Ryan, or perform in movies like Robert De Niro. Whereas balance usually applies to the functions of the physical form, Spiritual Balance applies to non-physical spirituality and aligns with such spiritual virtues as temperance, peace, fortitude, and patience. By maintaining Spiritual Balance in all things, we stay on a righteous spiritual path and rarely falter. Perfect Spiritual Balance requires energy that we can use to live healthy, peaceful, and productive lives, both on Earth and in our Afterlives. Spiritual Balance allows us to maintain consistent levels of temperance, patience, fortitude, calmness, kindness, and peace. This high level of pure balance is difficult on Earth, but not so difficult in our Afterlife."

One of the sparkling angels then changes from cerulean blue to magenta red, lights up like a Christmas tree, and continues, "Spiritual Balance, also known as Universal Balance, keeps us away from extreme thinking and living. When we take in too much or too little of anything, our physical forms, ego minds, and spiritual forms become unhealthy and suffer. When we worship idols other than Divine Energy or God, we lose our authentic and righteous spiritual path. When we become too much of one thing and not enough of the other, we lose track of the personal spiritual lessons we are learning. Without balance in our spiritual selves, virtues and moral values are lost. To be kind and spread love to the Universe, we must harness love and kindness in ourselves and suppress feelings of apathy, disgruntlement, and discontent. We must balance the energy of our emotions, desires, and practices to be One with Universal Energy and Universal Balance. Metaphysical and divine spiritual growth requires all humans and all spirits to learn the lesson of Spiritual Balance."

The two colorful illuminated angels advised me to return to Earth for a short while. They suggested it would be good for me to view some of my many past experiences on Earth. Viewing these experiences would illustrate how to balance all of life's experiences and challenges. I exited my comfortable lotus position and made my way down to Earth. It was lightyears away, but my journey was completed in an instant slither of time. As I left, I thought to myself, "Someone might see me leaving," but then I thought, "It probably doesn't matter."

Balance on Earth

Balance is the true essence of an enlightened life. Enlightenment on Earth may consist of both physical practices and spiritual life at the same time. Balance is dispersed fairly equally between worldly endeavors and spiritual growth. Extremes are fraught with danger around every corner. For example, alcohol in moderation is good to prevent ailments. In extreme cases of chronic intoxication, an alcoholic runs the risk of poverty and liver failure. Similarly, money helps pay the bills and allows for an occasional vacation. However, an extreme fixation on obtaining money at any cost leads to greed and crime. Alternating work and relaxation can be a balance that leads to happiness and success. Being a workaholic or a slacker leads to exhaustion, uselessness, and lack of purpose.

I have just arrived on Earth after having been given the explanation for Spiritual Balance by the two colorful and illuminating angels in my After-life. In my spiritual form, I hover over my church pew in Rosedale, Queens. The year is 1962. I am seven years old, my older sister is nine, and my older brother is fourteen. My younger sister is two years old. My mother and father stand next to each other, and my two-year-old sister is in my mother's arms. I get the laughter rolling. Soon, all of us kids burst into laughter for no reason at all. Once I start to laugh, it is so difficult for me to stop. The more I try to stop laughing, the more difficult it becomes to control. All of us kids look at each other, and this makes us laugh even more. Then my mother yells, "Knock it off!" and we immediately clam up.

Is my heart into what I am doing? Not so much. My younger spiritual self is lacking awareness, even though I am in the Catholic Church. I have not yet reached Spiritual Balance at this point in my life, as I am consumed by my ego mind and do not understand the importance of spiritual authenticity. I am young, but this day at church is a significant opportunity to grow my spiritual life—an opportunity that I missed. Church worship is an opportunity to give glory to God, but I fail him. I laugh during the church service because I do not take spiritual life and God seriously. I am more focused on temporal life than on religious life.

My early years consisted of a spiritual imbalance that was mainly aligned with my worldly life instead of my holy life. Now, I affirm that going forward, I will practice the spiritual lesson of Spiritual Balance in my life.

See yourself as a youngster in church or synagogue. Meditate on this, if you wish. What were you thinking and doing? What do you experience today when you go to church or synagogue? Or maybe you don't go to church or synagogue at all. Should you? What do you say when you pray? Do you pray?

I have never been a big proponent of organized religion. Much of it is fabricated by men and women. Much of it is superfluous and ungenuine.

For me, personally, my relationship with God is much more important than showing up for church services, even though I sometimes go to church. To have a good relationship with God, we can worship him both inside and outside of church. We can worship him at home, we can worship when we walk in nature, and we can worship in our day-to-day lives as much or as little as we want. I like to talk to God during the day. Sometimes, as ominous problems arise, I will ask God, "What do you think of this?" Sometimes, the answer comes to me from the Bible. Sometimes, his answer comes to me through my spiritual intuition. Sometimes, the answer does not yet come. I believe that by keeping a strong relationship with God, the Universal Energy of love and goodness, I am kept on a righteous path. Your spiritual state and spiritual growth may be different than mine; this is fine. Because I believe in the balance of the Universe and Spiritual Balance, I do not find it necessary to worship God at every moment of our lives. We must keep a balance between worldly things and ethereal things. Integrating the two simultaneously is always preferred.

I am now eight years old. I am all consumed with baseball, basketball, and football. No, I take that back. I also love other sports such as hockey on roller skates, wiffleball in the backyard, stickball in the schoolyard, fishing at a local pond, Frisbee anywhere, and the list goes on. As soon as I arrive home from school each day, I am ready to play ball. This goes on from about age seven all the way through high school. I play some college baseball as well. As I watch myself play football with my friend Joey in the streets of Laurelton, Queens, I wonder what my life would have been like had I, as a young boy, found more of a balance between sports, education, learning, my spiritual growth, and my relationship with others. What if my relationship with God had been stronger? If I could have balanced practical activities with spiritual growth in equal proportions, I would have been happier and probably more successful. I would have discovered a Spiritual Balance.

The year is 1980, and I find myself in the Manhattan Chess Club in New York City. I can see that my love for chess is all-consuming. On some weekends, I play speed chess for five or six hours in a row. On weekdays, I often play chess at night after work. I arrive home around ten o'clock at night and feel physically and mentally exhausted. I begin my medical studies but often fall asleep before they are completed. Essentially, I'm addicted to chess. If I'm not playing chess, I find myself viewing chess moves in my head and reading chess books that review classic chess openings and endgames. I have little desire and little time to do anything else. It is obvious that I have lost the ability to balance work and school with my chess life. As I look down from above, watching myself play chess on this day, I realize that at this time, I have no concept of the importance that balance, especially Spiritual Balance, plays in a person's life.

Fast forward to the year 2000. This is the year of the dot-com bubble. Prices of Internet and technology companies had been going straight up for about three years. Now, in the year 2000, the prices of these technology stocks begin to sink fast and furiously, and many Americans lose moderate-to-large fortunes. This is similar to the bear market we are experiencing in the United States today in the year 2022 (At the time of this writing, the NASDAQ stock index has fallen almost 30% off its highs.) But in the year 2000, companies like Cisco Systems, Microsoft, and Sun Microsystems have stock prices that fall to single digits. I am an inexperienced investor and hold onto these stocks, and other stocks like them, for much too long. I feel an empty pit deep within my gut that makes me feel like vomiting daily, as much of my life savings sinks away. My accountant tells me to hang onto these stocks because they are "good companies." He also talks about placing *put options* on the stocks, which I never do. These companies are like my babies. How could they ever hurt me? How could I ever let them go?

I should have sold sooner and because I didn't, I got hurt financially. At the time, I had invested almost exclusively in technology stocks. This experience helped me to learn the importance of financial asset allocation. Put simply, asset allocation is dispersing your investments into various types of investment holdings such as stocks, bonds, real estate, commodities, and others. When stocks are purchased, all stock market sectors should be purchased and not just those in technology. This balances one's portfolio so that, even in down markets, you lose less money—since not all types of investments go down by the same amount at the same time. In down markets, the individual who loses the least money is the winner. So, we can conclude that by diversifying our financial holdings, we are creating investment balance that produces more effective yield and better risk protection. Do not ever get emotionally connected to your investments This is an example of the importance of balance in the financial world. The bigger lesson is to never do anything extreme. Stay balanced in all facets of your life, including your finances. For me, this was learning a lesson 'the hard way.'

Balance is one of the most important lessons of life to live by. It can be seen in almost every facet of life, including finance (as we just learned), health, work, child-rearing, and much more. Excess food consumption (too much calorie intake) leads to obesity and poor health. Good nutrition is the balance of eating all the required food groups, including carbohydrates, lipids, and proteins. Caloric intake should be monitored to control both excessive consumption and malnutrition.

Individuals should always balance work with leisure. There is much truth in the adage, "All work and no play makes Jack a dull boy." Those who spend too much time at work are known as *workaholics*. Workaholics become obsessed with getting tasks completed, to the exclusion of their families and friends. When people work too much, their relationships suffer, and they miss opportunities to experience the world. Work should never have priority over health, love, education, spiritual growth, and life's purpose.

Raising children requires as much of your personal presence and guidance as possible. Unfortunately, many parents must put their children in childcare for a good part of the day. It is often non-family members that must help educate, guide, and fend for the child during early critical growth years. It is especially important to keep a balance between the parent's time with the child and daycare time, whenever possible. Child-rearing must also be a balance between discipline and allowing children freedom to decide.

Too much freedom given to a child will result in them making poor choices when they are too young to make appropriate decisions by themselves. Too much discipline will give them hopeless feelings of self-doubt and lack of freedom.

Think of the balance that exists both in the macroworld and the microworld we live in. Imagine the balance that exists between the stars, the solar system, the planets, and outer space. There is a perfect amount of gravitational pull on our bodies to keep us comfortably grounded to Earth. Forces of inertia and gravity between celestial bodies in space keep the astronomical Universe in continuous balance. Incredibly large as these forces of the Universe are, they nevertheless function in harmonious balance. Contemplate our planet, which is just a fraction of the entire Universe, with its balance in temperature, water masses, amount of sunshine, and consistent gravity, all functioning flawlessly to keep us alive. Antithetically, a world with excess carbon emissions is a *man-made imbalance*, which will lead to severe global warming and a dysfunctional ecosystem.

On a biological level, if we look at our physical bodies, we see an amazing balance of organ systems that keep us healthy. Our liver, spleen, kidneys, nervous system, and lungs all function in harmony with each other to keep us living well. On a cellular (micro) level, cytoplasm, mitochondria, proteins, along with our immune system and genetic code all function as One, in perfect balance, to allow for our good health.

Spiritual Balance

There is a Spiritual Balance of energy between our souls and Divine Energy. This bond constitutes the Spiritual Universe, which consists of temperance, faith, hope, love, mercy, charity, Oneness, enlightenment, and God. Additionally, patience, fortitude, calmness, peace, love, and kindness are all spiritual virtues that are a large part of the Spiritual Balance of the Universe. When our spiritual virtues and spiritual life are in balance with life's physical and mundane activities, we call this Spiritual Balance. It is important to maintain a balance between our physical mortality, our mental health, and our Spirit. For Spiritual Balance to be in equilibrium, it requires that we do not excessively ponder our spiritual self, physical self, or mental self. If we become fanatical about our spiritual self, our bodies and minds may suffer. Though our relationship with God is extremely important, God does not want us to ponder him twenty-four hours a day, seven days a week, to the exclusion of all worldly demands. He would prefer to see us function effectively in this world he created for us while enabling our spiritual virtues and Spiritual Balance to shine through in our actions. For instance, if a health-care worker gives his patient a difficult prognosis but delivers the message in a loving, Godlike tone, he balances his spirituality with performing his real-world (practical) job.

Imagine you have a neighbor who is elderly and is currently having a lot of difficulty walking. You have a busy day and need to quickly pick up groceries before going to an appointment. It is a Monday, and this is when your elderly neighbor does her shopping. She calls you right before you leave the house and asks you if you can pick up a few items at the store for her. She cannot get out of the house due to crippling leg pain. The timing is bad for you because you are on a tight schedule today; nevertheless, you agree to go out of your way and shop for her because you want to help her. Your actions of *giving* and *empathy* are spiritual as you perform the practical and productive act of shopping for both of you. Your actions exemplify being practical (getting the shopping accomplished) while practicing the virtues of compassion for your elderly neighbor at the same time. This is Spiritual Balance that pleases God.

Spiritual Balance as Seen from the Afterlife

I am dead, and I have been sent today by my illuminating angelic mentors in my Afterlife to learn more about how my life and other lives can be better served by living with Spiritual Balance. There is still time within our imaginations for all of us to die and see how we have lived our lives. These remembrances may help us become more spiritually enlightened and

Spiritually Balanced in our everyday thoughts and actions today. As we accomplish this, we will create more happiness for ourselves than we could have ever imagined. Spiritual Balance keeps us feeling secure because it is the least risky way to live. This balance keeps us from making big mistakes when there are important choices to be made. We are living our life in a controlled fashion without allowing life's extremes to take hold of us. When the Afterlife makes the events of our lives clear, we attain a Universal Wisdom regarding decisions to be made. Spiritual Balance creates happiness and peace for us and, collectively, for the greater good of humankind.

I am exhausted, and it is time for me to return to my Afterlife. I have reviewed a few challenging experiences from my early life in detail. I am filled with amazing feelings of spiritual nostalgia after seeing our young family again so clearly. I have closely examined my early passions and the lessons I learned that shaped the person I am today. I am also happy because I have come so far in learning the lesson of balance and Spiritual Balance in my everyday life.

Upon Returning Home

Upon returning to my Afterlife, I reflect on what I have learned about Spiritual Balance. Life on Earth is a balancing act. All day long, we must balance our thoughts, our emotions, and our desires with restraint. We balance our family life, work, social life, and our physical and spiritual worlds (Solomon). We must somehow live our practical lives and our spiritual lives at the same time.

I learned that Spiritual Balance is required for peace, fortitude, patience, and temperance. The keyword *temperance* especially came to the forefront of my consciousness. To have temperance is to have self-control over our ambitions, passions, and work (Wright). We can think of temperance as "all things in moderation." We must find an acceptable equilibrium between our practical life and our spiritual life. Successful living includes a balance between worldly obligations and time for worship and discipleship of God.

Sometimes, we must hold our deep worldly desires in abeyance to allow time for spiritual meditation and prayer.

Many Christians define Spiritual Balance as an equilibrium between worship, discipleship, fellowship, evangelism, and ministry (Warren 303-304). These are acts of devotion to God that Christians perform to bring pleasure to God (65). Others believe that these devotions and commitments to God should be done in moderation so that Christians and other religious followers can enjoy the worldly gifts that God offers. Many spiritual followers feel that they need time for recreation, hobbies, relationships, necessary work, and other responsibilities. As explained by Rick Warren, "You may feel that the only time God is pleased with you is when you're doing "spiritual" activities — like reading the Bible, attending church, praying, or sharing your faith. And you may think God is unconcerned about the other parts of your life. Actually, God enjoys watching every detail of your life, whether you are working, playing, resting, or eating. He doesn't miss a single move you make" (76). When we can combine our spiritual devotion with our passions and work and still maintain equilibrium (balance), life is extremely fulfilling.

What can you do if your worldly life and spiritual life are not balanced?

1. Read verses related to Spiritual Balance in the Bible.

2. Keep a journal and record your activities. Keeping a journal will allow you to recognize how much time you spend on spiritual growth.

3. Ask God to help you find balance in your life. You can talk and pray to God about keeping symmetry between temporal affairs and spiritual devotions.

4. Speak to your minister, family, or friends about keeping a Spiritual Balance.

5. Meditate on finding equilibrium and moderation in spiritual life.

6. Return to nature to find balance. When looking at living things in nature, you will see Oneness and Spiritual Balance in the relationships they have with each other.

7. Read a spiritual or non-spiritual book. Reading will often take your mind away from worrying about the stresses of balancing your spiritual and practical life. When you are feeling overwhelmed and stressed, diverting your attention to books and activities will make you feel better.

8. Create a balanced social circle. Your friends and acquaintances that you often interact with, including interactions on social media, should be chosen carefully so that both your mundane activities and spiritual activities are well-proportioned.

9. Work on changing your habits (Quinn).[1] Repeated activities in life are often done out of habit. When you find your life is out of balance, make note of those habits that are unnecessary or taking up too much of your time. Redirect your actions towards activities that create worldly and Spiritual Balance.

Affirmation: "I will focus on my priorities and will succeed without becoming extreme about anything."

---

1   Quinn lists several of the solutions 1–9 discussed here.

CHAPTER 6
Self-doubt and Our Spirit

I was looking for someone to inspire me, motivate me, support me, keep me focused...
someone who would love me, cherish me, make me happy, and I realized that I was looking for myself all along.

—Unknown

Self-doubt in My Afterlife

Floating on puffy white gas in an existential frequency, I begin to meditate. I have a crystal-clear conscience with zero feelings of self-doubt. I allow complete Spiritual Oneness to penetrate all of my most sacred intentions. My self-esteem is at the pinnacle of my being, as I enjoy every blissful moment of existence in my Afterlife. I look back at all the self-doubts and insecurities I experienced before death and almost laugh at how silly I was. I realize now, through my death, how much precious time I wasted while on Earth.

If I had really known that those times of fear and lack of self-worth were minuscule drops of time in the temporal spectrum of lifetimes to come, I could have lived so differently. With my eyes now wide open, I can't help but smile as I know I can accomplish anything I put my mind to just by following my heart.

How could I have been so afraid to take chances? Why did I constantly think I would fail? Why did I not feel worthy enough of success and financial gain? Why on Earth did I think so many things were impossible for me?

I stop all my thoughts while meditating. I return to an awareness of what breathing feels like while alive. Then I even let that go. At that moment, I "let go and let God." Total bliss permeates my being as I am wrapped in warm feelings of love and goodness. Everything now is so easy, as I realize I never had anything to worry about. There was never any need for anxiety, fear, or depression. When we remove self-doubt, we live with peace of mind and can truly live in the moment.

At that split millionth of a second, a family of angels surrounds me and emits the most brilliant glowing colors ever imagined. They communicate to me that I have learned my spiritual lessons well and that I am being considered as an entity who might be moved to the next Afterlife very rapidly. They tell me I should feel proud and that my soul's purity is so closely aligned with where I am at in my meditations, prayers, and higher consciousness. They want to celebrate my achievements with me. I ask them if we could wait until later to celebrate, as I want to write more about how people can overcome self-doubt. I also want to write about how all persons on life's journey could learn to repair their low self-esteem. The angels agree and affirm, "Good luck. We will see you later for the party."

Self-doubt

Self-doubt can lead to fear, anxiety, depression, worry, and loneliness. Self-doubt blocks us from acting. Long-term self-doubt can hamper our productivity and success. It leaves us frozen and unable to conquer life's challenges and obstacles. When we have self-doubt about our decisions, our actions, and our intentions, we lose confidence in ourselves.

When one has confidence instead of self-doubt, their *self-efficacy* levels may be extremely high. Self-efficacy means an individual believes in their own abilities to reach goals or tasks, meet challenges, and improve their skill levels (Dream Team. Personal Agency…). Self-esteem is the regard or respect that a person has for oneself. When individuals have strong self-esteem and confidence, their behavior becomes efficacious, and they can better control their plans of action and strategies. The degree to which people can make their own decisions and perform actions that control their own outcomes is referred to as *personal agency* (Dream Team). People become motivated, creative, and insightful, and they regulate all their cognition to create their desired experiences. With positive self-esteem, self-efficacy, and personal agency, individuals become more intentional, self-reactive, and self-directive. In this way, persons become less subject to life's whims and take ownership of directing their own actions to create their own destinies. Persons with a keen sense of personal agency and self-efficacy often have high levels of self-worth. These persons are better prepared for life's disappointments and adversities. As we learn to cope with life's heartaches, we become free of self-doubt and are increasingly capable of building positive self-esteem. We become confident and move away from self-criticism. Our "mind voice" or internal thinking becomes positive and empirical, ready to perform valuable tasks.

Self-doubt can begin at almost any age, including childhood. Self-doubt may occur when we fail at something, or it may occur after an accumulation of multiple failures. This is unfortunate because it is often failure that propels us to new and grandiose accomplishments. Those who are most successful in general are those individuals who learn from their mistakes and persevere. If we are unable to cope with failure, we will be overcome with self-doubt. When we work at spiritual growth, we learn that God loves us with all our failures and flaws. By internally speaking with the Divine Energy Source or God, we release our failures, fears, and self-doubts to the Spiritual Universe and replace them with self-efficacy and personal agency.

Self-doubt is also a result of negative words directed at us by others. A parent who is critical of their child instead of supportive may create self-doubt in him or her. It is extremely important that a parent give praise and accolades when their children do well at all achieved tasks. Accomplishments in things like school studies, music, art, chores, effective communication, and caring should all be rewarded.

Many people have great ideas but fail to act upon them, resulting in various losses. The person looking for employment who feels that he is unqualified for such a prominent position with a high salary loses the opportunity because he never sends out his resume. A wonderful singer that doubts his or her ability to sing in a higher octave never auditions for a dream role in the show and misses the opportunity, which with a little practice, they would have achieved. How many of us have said too many times to ourselves, "I can't do that," only to find out later we had missed a golden opportunity? Not trying, out of fear and self-doubt, is a death sentence to a golden opportunity lost forever.

A word or two about fear. It is often our fears that result in self-doubt. Fear leaves us with a poor self-image. When I am fearful, I am less likely to take a chance. I may be afraid of the outcome. Fear of damage or injury to either our physical self or mental self will have us question our abilities and talents.

It takes confidence to speak in front of those who we think know more than we do; we are afraid of their criticism. If we make a couple of bad plays on an athletic field, suddenly, our self-doubt entices us to quit the team. If, while looking for employment, companies continuously reject us, we soon begin to think there is something wrong with our qualifications. We are now fearful of applying for jobs because we want to avoid additional rejection. A saying attributed to William Shakespeare says, "Our doubts are traders, and make us lose the good we often might win, by fearing to attempt" (Perry). My mother used to say, "Have no fear. Ninety-five percent of what we worry about never comes to fruition. It is the other five percent that we never thought of that will get us." Fear must be overcome to eliminate self-doubt. Sometimes love will conquer fear. Remember that it is well accepted that "God is love." We can therefore say that God conquers self-doubt.

Writing this book, there were many times when I experienced both fear and self-doubt, and almost quit writing. I thought, "Who am I kidding? I don't have the knowledge to author this book. My thoughts are not clear enough, and my grammar is not good enough." When these uncontrollable thoughts burst into my mind like a violent assault, I told myself with strong conviction, "I must stop having self-doubt. I must persevere at all costs. I can do this." I had to give myself these commands (affirmations) many times during the writing of this book. Furthermore, I used my power of intention and the "Spiritual Law of Attraction" to complete this writing. I prayed on the success of my first published book. Finally, I imagined myself dead and looked back on my life with one completed spiritual book under my belt. When I did all this, I learned this wasn't all about me. My consciousness brought me to the reality that the living world needed this book. My higher consciousness made this book about spiritual virtue instead of satisfying my ego mind. Individuals will grow spiritually through this writing by losing self-doubt and fear of failure. They will begin to understand the causes of their lack of self-worth by augmenting their spiritual life skills. If more of us could live our lives with less self-doubt, more self-virtue, and more prayer and meditation, we would find purpose in the world and a better plan for how to live. As we use our spiritual tools and learn our spiritual lessons, we wash away self-doubt and become confident in ourselves and the world around us. Use the Spiritual Laws of Attraction and Spiritual Oneness to remove self-doubt in your life.

Self-doubt is characterized by negative thoughts and feelings about one or more aspects of ourselves. Self-doubt can lead to depression and debilitating consequences. To overcome self-doubt, we must develop tools and techniques to promote positive thoughts and feelings about ourselves. Firstly, we must not continually try to achieve things that are virtually impossible for us. This would be like repeatedly hitting your head against the wall, only to discover the wall never breaks, but your head will. If you are horrible at soccer, year in and year out, don't try out for the travel team. If you cannot carry a tune, stop trying out for *American Idol*. By being flexible, trying to reach goals that are attainable, and performing activities that you are good at, your self-image will blossom. Don't waste your time doing things that make you feel bad about yourself unless you absolutely must.

Stay away from those who criticize you, and most importantly, don't believe what they say. What someone said is probably intended for someone else and not for you. Spend your time with people who both like you and are supportive of you. These are usually loving family members and good friends. They will remind you of your talents and why you are so likable.

Recall your numerous achievements. Give yourself credit for your knowledge in certain areas where you excel. Remember and enjoy all your talents and give yourself credit for these. If you play tennis well, then play it more often. If you used to play tennis well, consider starting to play again.

Try not to compare yourself to others. There will always be someone else who does things better than you. It is about finding joy in the things that you do and not about someone else's ability.

If we want to live a confident life with a strong self-image, we must first be true to ourselves and live with intention. It is important to know your authentic self and your purpose in life. Reflect constantly on your spiritual self, and search for your soul. In this way, when you come to the end of your life, you will reflect on a life that followed a pure path drawn by your creator. When we open ourselves to our Spirit self, dreams, and aspirations, we live month-to-month and year-to-year, eventually arriving at old age true to ourselves. When we believe that our spiritual life is most important, we begin to find meaning in life, and our life takes on purpose. When we form an active relationship with God, we have found the purpose for our lives. We find the person we want to be and the purpose we were put on Earth for. When we are confident about our true reality, which is living life with the highest spiritual virtues and values, we approach our Afterlife without self-doubt or fear. Those who follow their spiritual hearts will find happiness through their life's endeavors.

The spiritual heart of the person who wants to give and heal others may work in the medical field. The person who wants to bring riches to the world may be enthusiastic about increasing the net worth of others by working successfully as a money manager or financial consultant. Following your passion and working a labor of love results in total loss of all self-doubt. Feed your soul what it wants, and you will find your true destiny.

My mom's life was an example to the world of a woman who followed her heart and listened to her inner voice, thereby finding her true spiritual life path. First, to me and my siblings, she was a loving, nurturing mom who always put her children's needs before her own. Many times, she made self-sacrifices to keep us happy. My mother's true calling was that of a protector and caregiver of children.

Let me give you an example. We had neighbors who lived down the block from us. The family consisted of two adult parents and one child named Jane. When Jane was an older adolescent, both of her parents passed away in the same year. Being the empathetic person that my mother was, she would often ask Jane to have dinner with us and encouraged her to spend as much time with our family as she desired. My mom did not want her to be alone and was concerned for her well-being. During those times, Jane spent many waking hours living with our family.

Another example was when my mom set up a nursery school in a neighbor's basement. My mother demonstrated her love and nurturing qualities for all those small children while their parents were at work. Many years later, when the nursery school closed down, my mom would take care of young children at the homes of moms and dads who went off to work each day. Once again, she nurtured these children with love and understanding, giving them an emotional base of security and confidence. Many years later, at my mother's wake, there were many young adults in attendance, mostly men and women in their twenties. I had no idea who they were. My sister told me these were some of the young children my mom had helped raise years ago, while their parents were working. I was utterly amazed that these people, after all these years, loved my mom so much that they attended her wake. Furthermore, when I talked to them that day, they impressed me so very much with their maturity. These children my mother had nurtured had grown into young, spirited, impressive adults with little self-doubt. That day at the funeral, we all wept because we loved my mother so very much.

She was the epitome of a mother's love for all her children. She possessed a motherly Oneness of love that she spread through the Spiritual Universe. That day, I watched my six-foot one and six-foot five brothers-in-law weep (which I had never witnessed before) over the loss of their mother-in-law, who had always made them feel like beloved sons. Rest in peace, Mom!

We must always be true to ourselves as a way to avoid self-doubt. It is also important to know that being true to others will result in avoiding our own self-doubts. The cliché states, "What goes around, comes around." When we send out truth to the world, others respond by returning truth to us. If others are interested in delivering truth to you, you will feel empowered, and this will destroy your own self-doubt. When you are truthful to others, people learn they can count on you. Having people believe in us will fruitfully build a confident personality. Sending truth outward, you add a personal value that transcends our mortality and brings us additional spiritual growth.

Do not believe it when people try to convince you that two views can both be right. In most situations, there is only one *truth*. The difficulty arises when we cannot find or prove the truth, because if we can't prove it, our adversary can take a different stance and proclaim they have the truth. For example, for centuries people have argued about the existence of God. The truth is that the believer and the agnostic cannot both be right. There either is or is not a God. The problem is we cannot prove this here and now. Down the road, when we reach our soul's final destination, we will then have proof of God's existence. Here is my list of Absolute Truths which may not be proven today, but you will surely believe when you experience Crossover to the Afterlife:

-You have been born and will be born again.

-You are living now and will live again.

-Your physical body will die, but you will not.

-At some point, you will live for eternity without pain and suffering.

-There is a God, and you will reunite with him.

People on both sides debate whether human life was created by the Big Bang or through God's deliberate act of creation. Even if we can scientifically prove that there was a catastrophic collision in space that led to the development of planets and life, it still may have been God who initiated the Big Bang. There is truth that exists, but we can't prove it yet. Later, when we ultimately reach the Kingdom of Heaven, Nirvana, or whatever term you choose, the truth will be exposed. Nevertheless, that one truth exists now; we just cannot prove it with empirical evidence. Sometimes, truth can come to us from others or from the power of the Universe. To some like myself, this truth can be sent from God to boost our belief in the cosmic Universe and God, resulting in less self-doubt.

I have always been shy about speaking in large groups and extremely uncomfortable with the idea of teaching a large assembly of people. About eight years ago, I was dating a lady who lived out of town. One Sunday, she decided to take me to her local Dutch Reformed Protestant Church. It was an incredibly special day at the church because what I will describe to you only occurred once a year at this particular service. Exactly one year before, church members had drawn from a hat a single word meant to represent a request from God, sent especially for each of them to act upon. On this day, volunteers could stand up and tell the church goers the impact the word had on them. Fascinating stories initiated by this word choice game were expressed by several members of the congregation.

One woman received the word *pray* the previous year. During the early part of the year, her mother, ill with terminal cancer, was given a three-to-six-month prognosis. Daily, this woman would pray for her mother's continued survival. Today, standing at the pew with her healthy-looking mother by her side, she told us that her mom was in complete remission. She attributed her mother's complete recovery to her prayers that were answered by God.

An elderly gentleman, let's call him Frank, stood up and said that his word was *charity.* The man said he was not one to donate money to charities. Since his word was charity, he uncharacteristically decided to donate $2,000 to the Make-a-Wish Foundation. As you may know, this foundation makes it possible for a chronically ill child to have his wish fulfilled. Frank said, "My money went to a child who wanted to see a professional NBA basketball game for the first time. I was asked if I would like to see the game with the child, and I accepted. A genuinely nice woman happened to be seated next to me, and we chatted with each other a lot during this game. At the end of the evening, I asked her for her phone number. Today, this woman is by my side here in church, and she is now my wife." Was the word *charity* really sent from God so that Frank could find a wife? Frank was sure of it.

Hearing many remarkable stories like these, I was anxious to pick "God's word" from the hat that Sunday morning. But when I pulled a word from the hat, it said *teaching*, and I immediately had ambivalent feelings because the idea of teaching brought up feelings of self-doubt. I put it in my pocket and said to myself, "I'll have to think about this one."

At this time, I was working in dermatology as a physician assistant and performed many cosmetic procedures, including laser therapy. When I went to work on Monday, I placed the yellow sticky note with the word *teaching* on my desk. On Wednesday, I saw the word *teaching* on the sticky note sitting on my desk, and I decided to place it high up on my bulletin board, above my computer. This way, it would be in clear sight and would reside above all the other sticky note messages. It reminded me that God wanted me to teach.

That day, an attending physician and a dermatology resident began to ask me about the procedures I performed. I told them about the various procedures I typically performed, and as I was speaking with them, I could tell they wanted to learn a lot more about laser therapy. When I got back to my desk and looked up at the bulletin board, I saw the word *teaching* and suddenly felt a compelling duty to teach the residents about lasers. I called the Chairman of the Department of Dermatology and asked if I could help proctor the monthly resident cosmetic clinic. To my astonishment, she immediately said "yes," and the rest is history. I taught the residents that year and had one of the most rewarding years of my career. Most importantly, I lost a lot of my self-doubt with regard to teaching groups of doctors. Through God's single word, *teaching*, the Lord had worked his magic through me.

Guilt

Guilt may result in self-doubt and low self-esteem. Guilt promulgates negative thinking, including worry and fear. Feelings of guilt can create a belief in self-inadequacy, which can result in emotional guilt.

Signs of guilt include but are not limited to anxiety, regret, nausea, insomnia, headaches, shame, lack of concentration, poor health, and isolation. Some severe cases of guilt or long-standing guilt may result in thoughts of doom, helplessness, and hopelessness. These individuals may experience lack of joy, since they see their circumstances as unfixable. They may even feel that they don't deserve happiness.

Some mild forms of guilt may be normal and are simply a sign of our healthy empathy and compassion for others. Guilt may be mild and easily resolvable, or it can be severe, with its cause and remedies extremely insidious. Guilt may be seldom experienced or perpetually dormant in the subconscious mind. It may also recurrently raise its ugly head, causing deep suffering to the guilty individual. Chronic guilt is often associated with other mental illnesses.

Guilt may be experienced for irrational reasons, such as when a person assumes responsibility for something they did not cause. *Irrational guilt* is usually associated with lack of self-compassion and lack of self-esteem, as well as feelings of inadequacy. Irrational guilt is based on "shoulds." We feel guilty because we should have done this or that, even though our decision may not be realistic or right. Irrational guilt can stem from irrational thinking, especially about consequences. When we go to play tennis, instead of staying home to play with our kids, we may feel guilty of neglect. *Rational guilt* is self-imposed and comes from violating our accepted moral values or standards (Taibbi). Rational guilt is considered rational when people cause harm to someone or create circumstances for which they are responsible. The individual may be responsible for poor choices and feel remorse.

There are many reasons that people experience feelings of guilt. Causes of guilt include anxiety, childhood experiences, culture, religion, and social pressure (Cherry "What is a Guilt Complex?"). People who have been criticized often as children tend to struggle with guilt as adults. As adults, they may experience shame, low self-esteem, and depression.

When a person feels they have treated someone unfairly, they may experience guilt. Some people who don't follow religious practices or cultural norms because of their individual views also may experience guilt. People can experience guilt because of transgressional thoughts that they may or may not have acted upon. *Survivor's guilt (Comparison guilt)* is a type of *existential guilt.* Survivor's guilt occurs when the guilty individual had a better outcome than those close to them. An example is when the guilty individual survives after a motor vehicle accident, but a family member in the same crash dies (Cherry. "What is a Guilt Complex?"). When a person feels their decisions and actions lacked righteousness and moral values, they will experience guilt. There are endless reasons why people experience feelings of guilt.

Fortunately, there are treatments for guilt. These include cognitive-behavioral therapy (CBT), other forms of psychotherapy, medication, meditation, and self-forgiveness. Connecting with God and His love will also treat your self-doubt. None of these treatments are foolproof, and they may take time to reach a good outcome. The first step in releasing guilt is identification by the individual that they are experiencing guilt. The next step is to find cause for the guilt. If the individual feels they have mistreated others, they need to apologize. Receiving forgiveness from others and forgiveness of oneself may be extremely helpful when seeking solutions. Forgiving yourself is important for your mental health (Cherry. "Taking the Steps"). When moral principles have been violated or transgressions have taken place, the individual needs to practice their spiritual lessons and live more righteously going forward. A review of good moral values may need to be rehashed and put into practice.

It may be healthy for the guilty individual to discuss the matter with family, close friends, doctors, and clergy members. Creating positive affirmations that address the causes of the guilt may prove useful. Prayer and meditation will give the individual a new perspective on the circumstances leading to guilt and the many solutions available. Sometimes, the individual may be exaggerating (in their ego mind) the events that made them feel guilty. Could they be "making a mountain out of a mole hill?" Could they perhaps learn how to accept these circumstances?

Through mindfulness and mindful meditation, a person who feels guilty can learn how to put their negative thoughts to rest. They can thereby replace guilty thoughts with positive thinking and intention. They can speak with the Divine Energy Source or God to find spiritual solutions. Through meditation and mindful review of all the circumstances leading up to the guilty event(s), they can harvest Universal Wisdom that will elicit solutions not otherwise thought of by the ego mind. When the individual utilizes the spiritual tool of higher consciousness instead of that of the ego (conscious) mind, they will better understand their guilt. By being creative, intuitive, and insightful, they will be given many opportunities to remove their guilt by themselves. If none of this helps, professional help is available. If professional help fails, then 'let go and let God.'

Meditation

Meditation treats a low self-image. Meditation is a treatment for a poor self-image, also known as low self-esteem. Meditation helps us to clear our minds and control our thoughts. We all have a voice in our heads, sometimes referred to as the ego mind. Without realizing it, our *mind voice* is always active with positive thoughts, negative thoughts, and neutral thoughts. It is those negative, prevailing thoughts that contribute to poor self-image. Poor self-image and low self-esteem occur when we don't value ourselves well. We question our self-worth. Negative thoughts about ourselves are unhealthy and can lead to feelings of uselessness, guilt, and depression. Through the spiritual tool of meditation, we can stop these negative thoughts about ourselves and begin to replace them with constructive, healthy thinking. Through meditation, we learn firsthand that our negative thoughts are not who we really are. Our authentic selves exude self-confidence and make us feel secure about our opinions and decisions. Our souls are our true selves and always see us as the Godlike entities that manifest our true reality. The goal of these meditations can be to improve our feelings of confidence and self-worth.

Meditation Exercise 1:

To start your meditation, pose in a sitting position with your spine straight. Close your eyes and relax all the muscles of your body. Now, make your mind as calm and quiet as you can. For a few minutes, pay attention to your breathing and nothing else. If a thought other than breathing comes into your mind, forget the thought, and return to the concentration on your breathing. Now, if you experience any negative thoughts about yourself, anyone else, or anything, recognize it, but don't identify with it. See those thoughts pass up into space and away forever.

See yourself looking at those unhealthy thoughts as an innocent by-stander. This is called mindfulness. From Chapter 4, we know that mindfulness is an intermediate level of meditation. You are aware of thoughts, but they are not part of you, nor are they you. Release all mental chatter that is critical or judgmental of yourself or someone else. If any ideas of poor self-worth enter your mind, visualize them being released into the atmosphere. When you have practiced this mindful meditation task for ten to fifteen minutes, you may stop the meditation.

If performed often, you will become good at this task and will bring only positive thinking about yourself into your everyday life's intentions. If this meditation is performed on a regular basis, your self-esteem will improve.

Meditation Exercise 2:

In another meditation endeavor, start the meditation the same way by getting into a relaxed position. Clear your thoughts, relax your muscles, calm your mind, and observe your breathing.

Now picture yourself in your local hospital. Imagine that you have severe chest pain and end up in the Emergency Room with a myocardial infarction. During this meditation, see your heart stop. Watch the health-care workers begin Cardiopulmonary Resuscitation (CPR) on your arrested heart. You are about to cross over into the Afterlife. See your Spirit lift out of your physical body. In that moment, see your whole life flash before your eyes. While meditating, visualize distinct images of the important events in your life. Pay particular attention to those events that allowed you to feel proud, worthy, and confident. Discover that you are not afraid. When your life events have finished, slowly come out of your meditation.

Now, think about all the most enjoyable, positive images that your mind's eye experienced while you were meditating. You'll find that at those wonderful times, you were true to yourself. At those times when you felt the most empowered, you were following your heart, your authentic intentions, and your keen intuition. You were listening to the voice of your soul.

It is important for you to realize that your happiness in those earlier times of your life was a result of your heart's desires and passions being aligned with your Spiritual Self, and you were fully confident. There was no self-doubt at that time. Enjoy yourself as totally confident. After spending time feeling empowered by your strong self-esteem, allow yourself to move to the next step.

While remembering the events seen in the previous meditation, ask yourself, "Since I survived heart failure, what will I do differently in my life? How will I regain or grow that powerful self-image and success I saw in those life images? Will I use my intuition and intentions to follow the spiritual desires of my authentic heart?" An unrecognized original source once said, "Today is a good day to die." This actually means that the person quoted is ready to die because they have no regrets. They have lived with purpose and a cause. Find confidence in knowing that you believe in yourself. If you have regrets, work on resolving these when possible.

Make your purpose in life to learn your spiritual lessons and live righteously. Develop your relationship with Divine Energy or God, and you will never doubt yourself or the life you have lived.

Prayer

If meditation is not your cup of tea, then you can replace it with prayer. Ask God to help you see your wonderful life images as if you were dying. It can be from heart failure or another illness, but you must envision your death as realistically and as clearly as possible. As you pray, talk to God about your self-esteem, both positive and negative. Ask God to help you find ways to grow your positive self-esteem and success today with the same positive self-esteem you felt while imagining your life's events. Tell God that you want to learn to live less in the flesh and more in the Spirit. You want to live by the spiritual virtues of honesty, faith, charity, kindness, and love. Tell God that you believe that your death is only a transformation to the Afterlife. Believe that experiencing your death will teach you how to live with greater spiritual righteousness. Tell God you will practice your spiritual lessons daily.

Affirmation: "Every day, I forgive myself and others for our transgressions, thereby releasing all guilt and becoming supremely confident."

CHAPTER 7
Higher Consciousness

You are the light of the world, when your compassion radiates and pervades the world. When your mind is in higher conscious- ness and heart is full with compassion, your deeds will glorify the humanity and the Father in the heaven.

—Amit Ray

Higher Consciousness in my Afterlife

Welcome to my higher consciousness in my Afterlife. My Spirit floats peacefully, completely free of all anxieties. Fear, self-doubt, and sadness are long gone.

I make my mind a clean slate using my imagination. Transgressions such as dishonesty, resentment, revenge, violence, pridefulness, narcissism, and hatred have long been annihilated by my higher consciousness. Won- derful spiritual virtues of love, kindness, giving, and forgiveness are who I have become.

I have total freedom now that I have shed my physical body. By using my heightened awareness, intuition, imagination, and insightfulness, there are no limits to the joy I receive on my ascending spiritual journey.

I am no longer at the mercy of Earthly life's whims. The Earthly roll- er-coaster of moments of triumph followed by deep sadness in its repetitive cycle has finally terminated. The brilliance of my higher consciousness in my Afterlife has destroyed physical and emotional pain.

I readily bond with Divine Energy or God as often as I want, and God always listens. God is my absolute best friend, and I do everything I can to please him. My worship of God is genuine and authentic, and God knows my love for him is pure and passionate.

I must tell you all how the rapture of the higher consciousness can be experienced while you are still alive. So, let me return to Earth now and tell you how you can live on Earth while experiencing your higher consciousness.

The Higher Consciousness on Earth

Higher Consciousness is a consciousness that transcends our ego minds. It may be considered metaphysical because it can transcend physical matter or the worldly laws of nature. Some believe that higher consciousness is an authentic reality, better than our normal state of ego consciousness. It is among our purest thoughts because we experience heightened awareness, much like meditation. It will often lead to spiritual growth since it can harvest Divine Energy and lead us to God. Persons can work at developing their higher consciousness, but sometimes higher consciousness finds them without their effort. Higher consciousness usually first occurs during meditation or prayer but can occur during existential activities or events.

When you use your higher consciousness, you may sometimes feel ethereal and connected to a Universal Energy. Your body may begin to feel physically energetic, light, and healthy. You may feel spiritually connected to nature, people, and the Universe. You may realize that all your thoughts are positive, and you feel incredibly optimistic.

People may ask, how else do I know when I am using my higher consciousness? When using your higher consciousness, you become more creative, aware, insightful, and intuitive. You easily find solutions to dilemmas or problems. Sometimes answers and solutions will be delivered to you without effort by Universal Wisdom.

You may feel more connected to the Divine Energy Source or God than you have previously. You will feel One with nature, people, and your spiritual path. You may experience spiritual virtues such as love, kindness, faith, charity, and more. You may feel like you are spreading love to the ecumenical people of all nations, to the souls in the world, and to those souls in the Afterlife. You may feel nostalgic and long for friends and family that are still living, as well as those who have crossed over into their Afterlife. You may talk to your Divine Energy Source or God about almost anything important or unimportant. You will have an unmistakable understanding that your spiritual self, and not your mortal self, is who you really are.

Materialistic desires and possessions will become less important than spiritual growth. You may find yourself devoting more time to prayer and/or meditation. On Sundays, you may choose church services, your local synagogue, or any place of worship instead of clothes shopping or wagering bets on sports teams.

You may focus on the spiritual lesson of *giving*. You may become a volunteer for causes that are dear to your heart. You will want to give more than you receive. You may start to donate money or time and find that this makes you feel incredibly good about yourself.

You will feel self-confident, knowledgeable, and wise. You will become less critical of yourself and feel worthy of all things. You will begin to feel your excellent self-worth. Your self-esteem will improve, and self-doubt will diminish. You will also become less critical of others.

You will see the abundance of the world and all it has to offer you instead of concentrating on scarcity in your life. In higher consciousness, you'll worry less about not having enough money because you will intuitively know that you'll always have enough. You have faith that the Spiritual Universe will be generous to you. You have the confidence that if you need something, you have the ability to find it on your own. If you cannot find it on your own, you know that with God's help, the problem will be resolved.

Your creativity and intuition will increase as you become more in touch with your authentic self. You will become empirical when it is necessary to find the truth behind an enigma. Otherwise, the scientific method will be less important than the metaphysical and spiritual worlds.

Honesty will be paramount to how you approach all of life's events. Your higher consciousness will deplete negative thoughts of dishonesty and iniquity. Your higher consciousness will always seek out truth.

It is important to speak a little bit about creativity since it is such a vital part of higher consciousness. Creativity is responsible for genius, medical breakthroughs, wonderful art, modern technologies, inventions, and much more. Happiness is derived directly from creativity, as well as from accomplishments that make us feel passionate and successful. Our creativity is a manifestation of who we are. Individualism is created as we identify with our specific talents. Where does anyone's creativity come from? It does not come from our physical form. It comes from our higher consciousness. It is usually nothing that is tangible. As we connect with our spiritual selves, our creativity blossoms. True creativity encompasses pure thought. Pure thought is concentration with laser-like focus. We cannot have this supreme level of focus while multitasking. People have become immensely proud of being able to multitask. Unfortunately, when we multitask, one or more of the things we are doing usually suffers. We cannot perform at one-hundred percent capacity when thinking of multiple things simultaneously. Text messaging while driving is an extreme example, but you understand the point being made. When we text while driving, our attention is diverted, and a car accident is more likely. When the higher consciousness is utilized, the task at hand is clearly seen, and all extraneous thoughts are abolished from the mind, encouraging the creative process to shine through. Higher consciousness is a state of high awareness that allows for greatest achievement with the use of creativity.

Higher consciousness is also known as *awakened consciousness.* Some Buddhists practice Asceticism, which is a practice of self-discipline. They believe in the principle of moderation and strive to achieve a higher state of being or awakened consciousness ("Asceticism"). Hindu sages talk about reaching higher consciousness through meditation and chanting. Some Eastern religions use terms like "awakened" and "enlightenment." In the book, *Change Your Thoughts—Change Your Life*, it is said Taoism "proclaims the Tao as the Way" to supreme reality (Dyer xiii). Christian monks practice silence to avoid sins, and it may also help them to reach higher consciousness. To some religions, higher consciousness is a tool to understand death and reincarnation. To others, it is a tool to reach Nirvana, defined as complete bliss.

For myself and others, higher consciousness is used to problem-solve in this world. It is also used as a tool to understand the Afterlife and eternal life.

Though many religions of the world talk about higher consciousness being ephemeral or temporary, I disagree. With experience, we can achieve a higher level of consciousness most of our waking hours. In the same way that we can talk to God as we move throughout our day, we can also maintain higher consciousness during daily activities. It is mostly a matter of maintaining keen awareness and staying pure in thought (positive thinking) while listening to our inner intuitive voice. This elevated state of consciousness allows our spiritual virtues to be practiced throughout our daily actions. We become immensely aware of practices of kindness, love, humility, respect, and our overall righteousness on a daily basis. We can repeat spiritually guided affirmations to ourselves as we go about the business of the day. One of my favorite affirmations, which I use almost daily, is: "For I can do everything through Christ, who gives me strength" (Phil 4.13). If you are not a Christian, use the affirmation, "I can accomplish all things today by maintaining goodness through the use of my higher consciousness."

Our higher consciousness will creatively find ways to overcome daily obstacles and setbacks. Higher consciousness will allow us to use more than just our creativity. Higher consciousness will also stimulate increased awareness, intuition, insight, and imagination. When creativity, awareness, intuition, insight, and imagination come from a state of higher consciousness, they may be referred to as *Spiritual Senses*. Spiritual Senses allow us to stay in the moment and avoid reflecting upon bad past experiences or negative outcomes. When the Spiritual Senses create *enlightened thinking*, Universal Wisdom is actualized, and we become analytical people known as *problem solvers*.

As we realize we are in this world, but not of it, worries and fears become disposable. The higher consciousness realizes that negative emotions and fearful thoughts are illusions, and they are quickly destroyed by our enlightened minds. Our view of the world and our reality slowly changes. Goodness, love, and kindness replace worry and fearfulness. The good moral values of our higher consciousness do not allow for continued animosity or resentfulness. We become grateful every day for our next breath, knowing with certainty that we were born lucky. We smile during the day and tell ourselves affirmatively that we are happy and joyous. No "sad news" or "bad luck" can destroy these feelings.

Spiritual Senses are more abundant and accessible in the Afterlife. The reason is that in the Afterlife, all entities have a much higher level of consciousness than mortal human beings do. In the Afterlife, we are no longer distracted by our physical forms. There are no aches or pains to divert us, and we never waste time pondering our physical presentation or attractiveness. Higher consciousness can speed us along a righteous spiritual path in this world, which leads to an evolved Spirit in our Afterlife. Higher consciousness helps us to learn our spiritual lessons now, leaving us with fewer lessons to learn when we Crossover to our Afterlife.

When I rest my head on my pillow at night, I clear my mind and create a blank slate. I am completely relaxed. Utilizing my highest level of consciousness, I begin to meditate. I say a meditative prayer and affirm to myself, "Life is good, and another good day will come tomorrow. Tomorrow I will utilize the Spiritual Senses of my higher consciousness to be happy and successful." Upon rising, I repeat this affirmation. In this way, my daily cycle of optimism through higher consciousness evolves in perpetuity.

Affirmation: "Through the use of higher consciousness, I will be creative, intuitive, aware, insightful, and imaginative to enhance my spiritual growth."

CHAPTER 8
Synchronicity and Spiritual Synchronicity

Life is monotonous if you don't allow for synchronicity. Through the years, I've learned that "chance" encounters aren't random. There are beautiful people and moments that can change your life if you let them. Synchronicity is the font with which God writes.

—Steve Maraboli

Synchronicity and Spiritual Synchronicity in the Afterlife

Three simultaneous, borderless, glowing, warm balls of light surround me this morning here in my omnipresent being of my Afterlife. Calm emotions envelop my total being that is everywhere. Three harps and three trumpets without distinctive connections to embodiments concurrently play Tim McGraw's famous song, "Live Like You Were Dying." Suddenly, the three indistinct balls of light turn into three beautiful celestial gas-like angels that lead me into a dreamland that looks like something out of *The Wizard of Oz.* The impressionistic court jester throws three celestial, white, fluttering illuminations resembling holy doves into the air, and they fly high and vaporize. Everything is here, there, and everywhere, because there is no time and space. Three non-minutes pass, and I hear the word "three" vibrate greatly in my being. The vibrations originate from where my ears used to be when I lived on Earth. I then realize I am experiencing three trumpets and three harps with no bodies attached, three formless angels, the word three, and three white fluttering holy doves in three non-minutes. This is obviously some sort of coincidence or synchronicity occurring before my very non-corporeal eyes. When the scarecrow who is only straw, the tin man who is formless tin, and a quiet, roaring lion appear, I realize I am dreaming of a distorted but beautiful "Oz." When the three characters in an all-encompassing vibrato squeak a high-frequency chant, "The Father, Son, and Holy Spirit," I have experienced the spiritual triad—and I find myself filled with creativity, love, Godlike awareness, spiritual power, kindness, and gratitude as my glorious day in the Afterlife begins. It is clear to me that there is a supreme Spiritual Synchronicity of three here in the Afterlife. Synchronicities on Earth were never this obvious. Either way, Spiritual Synchronicities are the Universe sending us messages through signs and symbols that we need to fulfill our spiritual purpose in life. You can learn this now, or you can learn it after you die. It's your choice.

Synchronicity and Spiritual Synchronicity

One of the Merriam-Webster definitions of synchronicity is, "The coincidental occurrence of the events (such as similar thoughts in widely separate persons or a mental image of an unexpected event before it happens) that seem related but are not explained by conventional mechanisms of causality; used especially in the psychology of Carl Gustav Jung" ("Synchronicity"). Psychologist Carl Jung introduced the term ego and the concept of synchronicity. He used the term synchronicity "To describe circumstances that appear meaningfully related but lack a causal connection" ("Synchronicity," *Wikipedia*).

Spiritual Synchronicity moves well past coincidence or chance. It can be viewed as an important message from the Divine Universe, sent intentionally to you for a significant benefit. The message sent to you may, for instance, solve a problem, bring you important knowledge, or help you to grow spiritually. In other words, part of synchronicity incorporates simultaneous events that have meaning to the individual or individuals involved.

Signs, symbols, and events all come together at the time we need them. Spiritual Synchronicity can seem like a small or large miracle. Our lives are speckled with meaningful synchronicities that we ignore or embrace and assimilate into our lives as spiritual nourishment for our soul. Spiritual Synchronicities have messages and reassure us that we are on the right spiritual path. Spotting, embracing, and interpreting these messages may be obvious or challenging.

What are some examples of Spiritual Synchronicities? Let's say Jane Love has been praying that she will meet a nice, spiritual man with whom she can share her life. She is coming home from work and reads a message on the subway that says, "So often we are lifted by old relationships that get revitalized." She doesn't think much about it and resumes habitual daydreaming on her commute home. That night, when she is watching a romance movie, David Kindness appears on the screen. Then, halfway through the movie, she views a commercial with a man named David. The next evening, as she arrives at her apartment door, her buried cell phone begins to ring in her purse. She fumbles with her apartment keys and finally gets the door open. She is digging in her purse to find her phone, and as the cell phone rings for the third time, she is certain the caller will hang up. But, as she slides the bar on the phone screen, she hears a voice say, "Hey Jane, this is David Faithful. I have been thinking of calling you for a while now. How are you?" Jane is stunned. She has not heard from David, a once close acquaintance, for about two years now. She is excited to hear David's voice because she always liked him very much. She has a genuinely enjoyable conversation with David. He winds up asking her for a date, and she accepts.

When the phone call ends, Jane repeats his name out loud several times, "Dave, Dave, Dave Kindness." Suddenly her thoughts go to the train message, "So often we are lifted by old relationships that get revitalized." Then she remembers the name "Dave" in the TV movie she watched last night. Finally, she gulps and misses a breath as she recalls that the name of the man in the commercial was also named Dave. She wonders if these messages foreshadowed Dave Faithful re-entering her life. Two years later, Jane Love and Dave Faithful are married.

This is an example of a Spiritual Synchronicity. Jane was single and had been praying that she would meet a nice man to share her life with. The two-time appearance of the name Dave, along with the train quote, were Universal messages sent to Jane to urge her to follow a path of love. After Dave Faithful called the very next day, it was obvious to her that all these events were more than just coincidence. To Jane, the messages were Spiritual Synchronicities, sent as gifts from the Divine Universe.

Let's look at another example of Spiritual Synchronicity—this time, a Spiritual Synchronicity from my own life.

After several intense arguments and one physical altercation with my father, I decided to leave home. I found a small room on the second floor of a stranger's house to live in. I was about to enter my third year of college at Hofstra University. My financial grants and other financial sources would not cover the tuition that was due. Because of the recent altercations with my dad, I was too angry with him, and too proud, to ask him for financial help. Eventually, I decided to take a year off and work full-time at a nearby liquor store—sixty hours a week—to save as much money as I could, so I would be able to return to college the following year.

As my working year progressed, I realized I would still be short by about $10,000, and my tuition was due in only a few weeks. I became fearful that I would never have enough money to go back to school, so I prayed to God every night that he would help me find a way to come up with the funds needed for my tuition. I entered into a deal or contract with God. I prayed to God that if he found a way for me to find enough money to return to school, I would never again doubt that he or his son Jesus exist. I also told God that I would live a spiritual life with great virtue and would go to church on a regular basis.

One morning, upon awakening, I heard the word *emancipation* in my head. Hearing this rarely used word, I was struck by its oddity. I tried to think of a time in the past when I might've heard this word. The only time I remembered hearing the word *emancipation* was when I was taught something in elementary school about a "Proclamation Emancipation" made by President Abraham Lincoln. Of course, this was the *Emancipation Proclamation*—an executive order made to free the slaves. I put to rest the word emancipation for the time being and brushed my teeth, took a shower, got dressed, and left for work. That afternoon at work, I went to the company cafeteria. The people at the adjoining lunch table were speaking loudly, and I heard a lady say, "I was trying to leave Russia, but it took the local government two years before they fully *emancipated* me." Wow. There was that word emancipation again.

I was watching television three days later when a commercial for B.O.C.E.S. college grants was playing. I went and looked up B.O.C.E.S. in the encyclopedia and found that B.O.C.E.S. was an acronym for *Boards of Cooperative Educational Services.* Since they were currently issuing New York State College Grants to those in financial need, I requested an application. When I received the application in the mail, I looked for the section for eligibility. To my shock, in bold letters, there was the choice for **Emancipated Individuals**! I couldn't believe it, because days prior to this, I had awoken to this very word and had also heard the lady in the cafeteria use it. I quickly got out my dictionary and looked up the word *emancipation* to confirm the definition. I learned that in a legal sense, emancipation (pertaining to this college grant application) meant a minor is freed from control of his parents or guardians and the parents or guardians are freed from the financial responsibility of their child. I filled out the application, checked the box "Emancipated Individual," and eventually received a $9500 grant (which did not have to be paid back), which allowed me to return to college. The money I received was almost exactly the amount of money I needed to return to school.

In reflection, I believe that the appearance of the word *emancipation* was more than a coincidence. I had been resolutely praying that I would find some way of getting the money I needed to return to college. I am certain that God answered my prayers. This introduction to the word emancipation was all too propitious to be explained by simple coincidence. I conclude that my experience was a Spiritual Synchronicity. The Universe revealed to me three separate *emancipation* word events that occurred almost simultaneously. Thankfully, I discovered their monumental purpose for coming into my life. I believe I received the money for college because Universal Energy or God granted me my wish. To me, this is a miracle of Spiritual Synchronicity.

It is amazing that God responded to the deal or contract that I had offered him. I have since learned that what God likes most is when we please him. We please God by surrendering our life to him and loving him with all our heart and soul. We do not please God by entering into deals and contracts with him. Maybe because my intention was so genuine and heartfelt, God answered my prayer despite the deal I offered him.

Coincidence is a remarkable occurrence of events that happens at or around the same time, which by chance are similar to each other. If I text John Doe and John Doe texts me at about the same time, we think of this event as a coincidence. With coincidences, there is usually no cause found. Synchronicity is similar to coincidence except that it is believed that the events are not by chance, but rather, they are meaningful and with purpose in our lives (Hopcke 17). Synchronistic events are not accidental, but rather indicative of an energy supplying a meaning or answer bigger than ourselves. This message may be from Universal Knowledge or some other Energy Source you attribute it to. In Spiritual Synchronicity, the simultaneous similar occurrences are sent from the Divine Energy Source or God to systematically bring us a life-changing impact.

Coincidence and basic synchronicity are usually considered to be acausal occurrences. In other words, the individual does not discern cause and effect (Hopcke 23). Neither the individual nor the players involved are seen as intentionally causing the remarkable simultaneous occurrences that stir the emotional experience. Spiritual Synchronicities usually involve simultaneous remarkable events that the individuals believe are caused by Universal Energy, Universal Knowledge, or God. Both simple synchronistic events and spiritual events consist of signs and symbols and occur at important transitions in our life. These events usually solve life problems or have special meaning to us.

Sometimes our inner world of thought, emotion, and need become simultaneously converted to an external world symbol or sign that brings helpful meaning or transformation to our lives. In this way, we alone do not determine the direction our life's path will take. Rather, the Universe may sometimes find and determine the necessary path that we have been seeking.

If Mary is troubled by mounting bills over a period of months, the Universe may send her signs or symbols regarding a solution. If she dreams about a work-at-home job as a domestic child consultant, her wish may be answered. The next day, two friends call her asking if she would like to be paid for taking care of their children while they go to work. This might be considered a coincidence, or more likely a synchronicity.

Let's say Mary goes to church two days later, and the sermon is from Proverbs, "The Godly walk with integrity, blessed are their children who follow them" (Prov. 20.7). Another passage read by the priest that day is also from Proverbs: "Even children are known by the way they act, whether their conduct is pure, and whether it is right" (Prov. 20.11). Mary may feel that God is confirming that her path to money is to become a caretaker for her friends' children. In light of her dream to become a caretaker and her friends' request for her to take care of their children, Mary has experienced a synchronicity. Since Mary believes the synchronicity was delivered by God, this would be considered a Spiritual Synchronicity.

It is the individual's own interpretation of the simultaneous occurrences that determines if this is coincidence, synchronicity, or Spiritual Synchronicity. These occurrences are usually private to the individual, and they themselves will determine the nature of the causality. In Mary's case, the events are highly life-changing and meaningful. Most of us would agree to categorize this as a synchronicity rather than a coincidence or accident.

We may or may not agree that this was a Spiritual Synchronicity because we have different opinions about whether God had a hand in the outcome. Synchronicities are deeply emotional and meaningful to the individual. Furthermore, it is usually the individual that decides whether the synchronicity is spiritual in nature.

I believe that synchronicity and Spiritual Synchronicity can both help change our lives in wonderful ways. For this to happen, we must be open to it. We must look for signs and symbols from the Universe and increase our awareness of the meanings behind experiences. Spiritual Synchronicities will show themselves when you have an intense problem, or you need and look to God for answers. They are likely to show up during or after prayer, meditation, intuition, or clairvoyance. As we relax our ego and calm our inner voice, we begin to hear and see the meaningful signs that culminate to deliver us on the path we are looking for. To find Spiritual Synchronicities, look for repeating numbers, recurring patterns, and repeating events or signs.

Study all of your dreams after waking up each morning. Significant events in your dreams may be synchronistical links to occurrences about to unfold in your waking life. Frequent dreams about falling in love may lead to real-life romance.

When interpreting occurrences and messages, rely on your intuition or "gut feelings." Listen to your inner voice, especially if you feel you can count on it. Listen to what life is presenting to you. The Universe always gives you exactly what you need, no more and no less. Each daily occurrence and person you encounter are there for you to behold; there are no accidents. We live in a perfect world that has an abundance of what we need. Increase your awareness of all the tools and solutions at your disposal. Incorporate the Law of Attraction. As you know, the Law of Attraction is a universal belief that man's positive thoughts or intentions will attract an equally positive result or reality. The person attains what he desires by visualizing and emotionally experiencing the feeling of already being in possession of the ultimate prize. We can use the *Spiritual Law of Attraction* philosophy by using spiritually righteous requests to attain Spiritual Synchronicity. We must affirm to ourselves that wonderful simultaneous occurrences are available to us through spiritual Universal Energy that sends signs from people and from nature. These signs are evidence to us of the spiritual path God wants us to follow. Using prayer and meditation, we can focus on all our important, virtuous aspirations. When we visualize and emotionally experience all that we desire, Spiritual Synchronicities will appear and allow prayerful wishes to become reality.

Synchronicity and Death

Exercise 1

Sit comfortably in a chair or lie on your bed. Relax all the muscles of your body and release all tension. Try to clear your mind as much as possible. If you already meditate, or if you began to meditate while reading this book, then conduct this exercise while meditating. If you do not wish to meditate while performing this exercise, that is fine as well.

Think back on the events of your life and try to find or remember any prior synchronicities you may have experienced. Try to see how your personal synchronicity may have altered the direction of your life. Did it involve love, pregnancy, a job, or death of a loved one? Did the synchronicity lead to a better place in your life? How do you identify it as a synchronicity based on the occurrences at the time? Do you believe God's hand was involved? Was the occurrence so unique and otherwise "impossible" that you had to believe the Universe worked to help or hinder you? Try to answer all these questions. If you had multiple synchronicities, then contemplate them now.

Exercise 2

Sit comfortably in a chair or lie on your bed. Relax all the muscles of your body and release all tension. Try to clear your mind as much as possible. If you already meditate or have begun to meditate while reading this book, then conduct this exercise while meditating. If you do not wish to meditate while performing this exercise, that is fine as well.

Your next exercise is to imagine and visualize synchronistic events that have not happened yet. These are about to happen in your future. This exercise will help you to develop your psychic sixth sense. You will use your intuition and imagination and will better develop an insightful aptitude. Spiritual extrasensory prediction is what you are striving for. These can be synchronistic events or Spiritual Synchronicities. Apply the principles of synchronicity that you have learned in this chapter. How will you be open to synchronistic events in the future? Do you think you will recognize signs and symbols when the Universe presents them to you? Will your synchronicities involve numbers? Will they involve a love relationship, a job, or a large purchase? What signs and symbols will be present, and in what meaningful way will your life change? See your favorite colors, favorite numbers, most memorable dates, and favorite people in your synchronicity. Who are the people who will interact with you in the Spiritual Synchronicities that will take place in the future? Try to answer all these questions by letting these answers enter your consciousness or higher consciousness. By allowing your thoughts free reign and keeping an open mind, your soul's connection to Universal Energy or God will help you visualize the life-changing synchronistical occurrences that will help you reach your desired goals. See clearly what you want, but more importantly, what God and the Universe wants for you.

Exercise 3

Sit comfortably in a chair or lie on your bed. Relax all the muscles of your body and release all tension. Try to clear your mind as much as possible. If you already meditate or are beginning to meditate while reading this book, then conduct this exercise while meditating. If you do not wish to meditate while performing this exercise, that is fine as well.

Perform a similar exercise, but this time you are dead. You realize that you have crossed over to your Afterlife. Think about the month, day, and year that you will die. Is your death 20, 30, or 40 years from now? Have you accomplished everything you wanted? Will you be cremated or buried? Do you have any regrets about not doing certain important things while you were alive? Have you apologized or come to terms with your adversaries? Will your siblings be alive or dead when you die? What will be the Spiritual Synchronistic events surrounding your death? Who do you hope will be there at the moment of your death? Will there be coincidences or Spiritual Synchronicities surrounding your time of death? Will you die on the day your mother was born? Will you die on the same day as your favorite number or a time of day that is meaningful to you? Will there be three, four, or five simultaneously related occurrences that will happen around the time of your death? Mark Twain was born in 1835 when Haley's Comet was seen in the sky. He died 74 years later when Haley's Comet was seen again entering the atmosphere. It is believed that before he died, he said that his death would occur when the comet reappeared.

When the exercise is over, consider that your answers may become your reality in the future. You may want to make some changes in your life based on your answers to these questions.

Conclusion

Everything you become aware of is delivered to you with heightened perception and emotion when you see that you have died. Look back on the choices you made while alive, and observe the responses you had to life-changing events. At the moment of death, calmness and clarity stimulate creative synchronicities. These meditative exercises will help you to readily become aware of synchronicities as they present themselves to you in the future. Furthermore, you are more likely to discover new knowledge about yourself from the synchronistic experiences that you reflect on and experience while meditating. See if you are able to realize some of the signs that God has been sending to you through Spiritual Synchronicities. He created these specifically for you. Performing the same exercises multiple times in the future will allow new Spiritual Synchronicities to become readily available. These exercises will also enhance your knowledge of your true self. They will help you realize actions you should take prior to your demise.

Try to see clearly what you desire. You have a plan in your life, and the Universe has a plan for you. The plan of the Universe will show up in your synchronicities and Spiritual Synchronicities. You do not have to control everything in life because the Universe has a plan for you. Do not fight, argue, or refuse to accept all that life brings your way. The Universe and God have a spiritual plan for us that has purpose. See what the Divine Energy Source or God's plan is for you by using meditation and prayer, your intuition, and your imagination. In this way, you will actualize many Spiritual Synchronicities that will inspire your spiritual growth.

It is through death—real or imaginary—that our heightened senses and keen awareness allow us to become one with our past, present, and future synchronistic messages. Our elevated spiritual emotions at the time of our death encourage us to see all that we have done in our lives, and all that we should be doing in our future.

Affirmation: "I am totally aware of the simultaneous clues and signs of the Universe, and I will use them to find my true destiny."

CHAPTER 9
Oneness and Universal Oneness

The noblest men of all ages, Christian saints of the most tran-
scendent spirituality have attained their wonderful development
through the spiritual rays of this planet because of the intense
feeling of Oneness with the divine and with all that lives and
breathes in the universe.

—Max Heindel

Oneness in My Afterlife

Enveloping me was my awareness of gray illuminations that reminded me of shadows on a partly cloudy day in the living world. I was beginning to sense a minuscule feeling of nostalgia when my deceased father's being infiltrated mine. I wasn't sure, because his physical form was dreamlike and distorted, but I believe he was wearing his police uniform. When I told him I had been searching for him from the start of my Crossover, he became like his Earthly self and retorted in his entirely familiar way, "Well, Michael, I've been here the whole time," as if to say, you really couldn't have missed me, had you really been looking. I started to feel a little defensive and annoyed, the way he often made me feel while on Earth, but the positive energy of the Afterlife removed these feelings almost immediately. I didn't even know it was possible to feel annoyed here in the Afterlife, up until now. I told him I missed him and was really glad to see him. I knew he was glad to see me, too. He did express that he was surprised to see me as if, in a fatherly way, he was expecting I would live on Earth forever.

I said, "You know, Dad, I was eighty-six when I passed away."

He replied, "Were you? I thought you were younger. Got to go now. Supposed to learn about Oneness today."

Then he left abruptly. I would normally be hurt by this, but this was the Afterlife, and bad feelings were close to impossible. I figured I might see him again soon, anyway. I felt really good that his spiritual lesson here was Oneness because his relationships with our family members had often been very hurtful. Nevertheless, I was elated that he was doing well.

Clarabelle, an angel I knew well, appeared and let me know I was needed. She wanted me to go with her to visit an entity, someone who was also struggling with the spiritual lesson of Oneness. In particular, he struggled with separatism.

Clarabelle and I left and found ourselves immediately in front of Noah, an entity who found himself more interesting than anyone else. His higher consciousness was still grappling with the human faults of lack of humility and separatism carried over from his Earthly life.

Clarabelle started communication with Noah with the question, "Why is it that you take so little interest in other souls? Do you not know that your true self is a part of the whole of the Oneness of the Universe?"

Noah forced himself to respond, "I know this intellectually, but I am unable to care for and give to others because I have a poor self-image."

I chimed in, "Noah, you have been created in God's image. Since you are One with God, you are divine, and therefore, your poor self-esteem means you are not aligning yourself with God."

Just then, Clarabelle declared, "Meditate or pray to God to show you that you were created in his image and therefore possess all Godlike qualities." Noah said he would do so immediately. I reassured him he was not

alone, and that Clarabelle and I were his sister and brother and would support him until he found Oneness with us and with God. Then Clarabelle
smiled and said, "There is a good party tonight at God-Town Seven. Both
of you dudes should come. It is going to be a really fun time." We agreed
and all dispersed.

Oneness in the Universe

Oneness is the connection that each human has to all living things, includ-
ing themselves, animals, society, countries, humanity, nature, and the Solar
System. If we add to this list our spirit, soul, and Divine Energy Source or
God, then we have Spiritual Oneness, commonly called Universal Oneness.
Universal Oneness is the connection that our physical form or individuality
has to the metaphysical world and to divine spiritual eternity.

The opposite of individualism is collectivism. Whereas individualism
or separatism disassociates one from society, collectivism bonds us with
society. Oneness incorporates both our individual and collective selves. As
an analogy, golfing is an *individual* sport (individualism), whereas baseball
is a *collective* team sport (collectivism). Both baseball players and golfers
are athletes (Oneness); whether they play an individual sport or a collective
team sport, they are still part of the world of competing athletes (Oneness).
To be clear, as individuals, we are part of Oneness—which is analogous
to being an individual and part of a family at the same time. In our lives
as human beings, we all experience both the feelings of being "alone" and
feelings of being "all one." As Dr. Wayne W. Dyer accurately points out in
his chapter on Oneness in his book, *You'll See it when You believe it: The
Way to Your Personal Transformation,* only one letter—the letter "l"—sep-
arates the words "all one" and "alone." He says, "this letter 'l' stands for
love" (119).

Please imagine yourself stranded on a desert island. It is almost certain
that you will never return to civilization again. You would begin to feel so
lonesome and isolated that you might feel close to a mental breakdown. You

would crave other people's company and yearn for a return to family and society. This example stresses the importance of Oneness with the whole of humankind. As the old adage teaches, "No man is an island." In the Bible, there are approximately thirty-five verses that point to the principle of two or more persons being better than one by themselves. One example of this is found in the Old Testament. Ecclesiastes says, "Two people are better than one, for they can help each other succeed. If one person falls, the other can reach out and help. But someone who falls alone is in real trouble. Likewise, two people lying close together can keep each other warm. But how can one be warm alone? A person standing alone can be attacked and defeated, but two can stand back-to-back and conquer. Three are even better, for a triple-braided cord is not easily broken" (Eccl. 4.9-12).

Sharing information with each other can keep us out of harm's way. Recently, there was a mass shooting in a Brooklyn subway station. Immediately after the shooting, the police posted a picture and description of this man. When the alleged suspect walked past a bystander in the street, the man recognized him from the police description and notified the police department. The police then arrested the alleged suspect and brought him into custody. It was the communication between the police, the public, and the alert man that led to the suspect's arrest, thereby establishing public safety. A civilized society is one in which people communicate well and become unified in Oneness.

Another reason Oneness is important is to combat global warming. All countries must work together to reduce carbon emissions. It will require the cooperation of all countries enforcing ESG (Environmental, Social, Governance) criteria as a set of standards to keep the world safe from the deadly effects of global warming. The countries of the world must work as a whole in Oneness to be effective in battling the tall order of climate control.

When individuals unite to become communities and nations of the world, we live as a whole, or a totality, known as Oneness. In this way, we are a "brotherhood of man." The concept of "brotherhood of man" reminds me of the Biblical question, "Am I my brother's keeper?" This is from the Bible story of Cain and Abel.

In Genesis, "Cain attacked his brother, Abel, and killed him. Afterward, the Lord asked Cain, "Where is your brother? Where is Able?" "I don't know"" Cain responded. "Am I my brother's guardian?" (Gen. 4.8-9b)

Cain was really saying, "My brother is not my problem." But God believes we are all to be each other's keepers (guardians). We should love and protect our families, brothers, sisters, and all of humankind. We are also told to "Love your neighbor as yourself" (Matt. 22.39). When people are hurting, ill, financially broken, or struggling in any other way, we should pray for them and assist them. God entrusts us to keep each other well and safe, thereby becoming our brother's keeper. As God loves each and every one of us, we are to love each other. When we need a brother's keeper to watch over us, those who love and care for others will come to our rescue. Showing love for our family and neighbors is one of God's commandments, but it is also the essence of Universal Oneness.

In this day and age, we can become One with the world more easily than ever before with social media and fraction-of-a-second communication services. Smart phones and computers allow us to communicate by email and messaging. The world is truly connected and global in a way that means news is shared almost instantaneously. The benefits of social media and the World Wide Web make the practice of Oneness and Universal Oneness available to us.

In Oneness, we are all held accountable to each other, the Universe, and to God. Realizing Spiritual Oneness and actualizing collectivism will make us a more peaceful and loving humanity. When we all do our part to share love, kindness, and respect with one another, a resultant collectivism of Universal Energy lifts all humanity to a higher spiritual consciousness. Additional unification of all individuals in communities, cities, states, and countries results in a summation of positive energy and Universal Oneness. In this way, the totality of humanity thrives and flourishes.

On the other hand, if we generate separateness by creating barriers to human communication, we forge a self-destructive path. The principles of

Universal Oneness are resisted by many people in several ways. There are those who protest others who are not like themselves by disregarding other races and nationalities. Prejudice and bias encompass an anti-Oneness that perpetuates a destructive decisiveness. Labeling other cultures, having enemies, and treating others with disrespect destroy a necessary unity of humanity. Creating wars, stealing land, and creating geographic boundaries are roadblocks to Oneness. Lack of harmony and instituting separateness among peoples and countries abolishes security among persons of our planet. We cannot feel safe when we know we are surrounded by potential enemies.

As countries blame each other for differences instead of working in unison to find peaceful solutions, the beauty of Universal Oneness is undermined. All humanitarian world leaders believe in working together toward the Oneness of world harmony and peace. These are the leaders who are completely opposed to using "weapons of mass destruction" or attacking other countries with chemical weapons. These leaders are responsible for forming the North Atlantic Treaty Organization (NATO), as well as The United Nations. Similar organizations include the European Union (EU), the World Trade Organization (WTO), and the Group of Twenty (G20). Effective leaders want peace and prosperity for people of all nations and don't wish success for their own country at the expense of other countries. Unity in world leadership is paramount for humankind to thrive.

War and killing are extreme examples of aggressive behavior of separatists that lead to human death and annihilation of man. Jesus said, "Love thy neighbor as thyself." Those leaders who start wars refuse to work in cooperation with countries that have different viewpoints and needs.

A leader who heads a dictatorship, who has no regard for Oneness or Universal Oneness, has neither respect for his own people nor the people and governments of other nations. An example of this is when the president of one nation creates an unprovoked war on an innocent country of people. The dictator murders and tortures innocent people, including women and children, and inflicts pain and suffering at will. These horrific leaders are narcissistic separatists who selfishly go after whatever they want. Mass murder and the use of weapons of mass destruction demonstrates a total lack of respect for the equality of all humans and a complete absence of concern for human life. I believe that when dictators invade other countries to annihilate and steal their land, the spiritual solution is to remove these dictators from office. NATO countries should unite and have these nefarious dictators removed. As I wish no man harm, it would be best to remove these vicious dictators and place them in controlled exile, as was done to Napoleon.

Oneness is a concept that involves the building blocks of life: the smallest parts of cells, bacteria, viruses, and the largest parts of outer space, including planets, stars, and galaxies. All the integral components from cell life to the solar systems of the Universe work together in perfect harmony and balance with one another, providing for the continuation of life. The cells of organelles function together as one viable unit. The many types of cells in our bodies, such as muscle cells, neurons, liver cells, pulmonary cells, and cardiac cells, all work in Oneness. Our organs all function simultaneously in a programmed way, thereby sustaining life.

The gravitational pull of the Sun on the planets and the gravitational pull of planets on their moons keep our solar system moving in perfect synchronization. This impeccable balance and compatibility between the workings of the tiniest cells, our physical bodies, and the cosmos constitute the totality of Oneness. All of nature, including the Animal and Plant Kingdoms, function harmoniously with man, the galaxy, and each other.

We all have heard of the "Circle of Life." A carcass of an animal decomposes and becomes the carbon nutrients needed for plants, trees, flowers, fruits, and vegetables to grow. The fruits and vegetables become a food source for man and animal. The oxygen released by plants and trees becomes the gas most living things, including ourselves, need for adequate pulmonary function and cellular respiration. The carbon dioxide that we emit by exhaling is utilized by plants and trees in a process known as photosynthesis, which is required to maintain plant life. When the trees and plants emit oxygen again, we have a complete cycle. In this way, all forms of life need each other and are connected in Oneness.

If it were not for the healthy bacteria we have in our gut, our digestive system would fail. Without good bacteria, our immune system would not be supported, and inflammation would harm our bodies. This entirety of cooperation on every level of existence in the Universe is the miracle of Oneness in life.

Let us look at how Oneness applies to the progression of life from birth through mature adulthood. The embryo starts in the mother's womb, where it is well-protected for about nine months. This is a symbiotic relationship in which the mother has all the conscious awareness. The mother is consciously aware of the life growing in her uterus, but the embryo has no conscious awareness of the mother. The mother is an individual that has Oneness with the fetus.

The baby starts life connected to the placenta by the umbilical cord. The umbilical cord is severed by the surgeon, and the baby becomes dependent on its mom for food and protection to sustain life. The baby knows little about his individualism, because he is not yet able to feel separatism. His own awareness is limited and open to discovery. Years later, the baby learns he or she is physically separate from mom, and the mother-child bond begins to change. For the first time, the baby becomes aware that he is physically separate from his mom but still very bound to her in Oneness. When he cries because he is hungry or needs to be held, he still immediately looks for his mother to satisfy his needs.

As the baby develops into a child, he is obsessed with his own life and soon begins to realize that he can do more things independently, without his mom's help. The individualistic side of his personality is forming, yet he still has a close bond of Oneness with his mother. The child goes on to become an individual who recognizes that he is separate and self-sustaining. He will keep that part of Oneness for the rest of his life.

Small children, older children, and adolescents learn to share with others and begin to learn cooperation and collaboration with all living things. They are also learning that their thought processes or minds are capable of many things beyond their physical selves and the physical world. Their thoughts become as important as their physical well-being. Their thoughts, created by their minds or consciousness, can bring them either boundless joy or fear and unhappiness. They know they are individuals but also realize they are connected with the world around them. They become mindfully aware that their thought processes can be trained to do what they like. A healthy body and a healthy mind are both needed for happiness and success. At this point, the self is creating a bond with all living things and the Universe.

Moving toward adulthood, when consciousness is further developed, a person's intention, creativity, insightfulness, intuition, synchronicity, and enlightened awareness can help them achieve almost anything they desire. At this point, Oneness represents the combination of a person's physical self, emotional self, inner voice or ego mind, and his or her spiritual awakening. This is the beginning of Universal Oneness, which encompasses the importance of one's spiritual self.

Towards the end of the Oneness maturation, a person loves himself, loves others, loves nature, and loves God. He sees himself as part of something much larger than himself. He is part of a Divine Energy Source that the Spiritual Universe shares with all of us. The person now makes their spiritual development a priority over material conquests. He is now One with the Universe: a component of Universal Energy and one of God's children. He feels genuinely connected to higher conscious awareness, people and emotions, nature, and God, which make up Universal Oneness. He is not alone, but rather is a co-creator with God or Divine Energy.

We are the product of the DNA, knowledge, wisdom, and emotions of all those persons who came before us and all those who will come after us. Universal Knowledge and Universal Wisdom are passed on from generation to generation. We realize that we are all the same and all part of the whole of humankind. The God that we worship, whether we call him Abraham,

Jesus, Mohammed, Gandhi, or Divine Energy, are all God. We will all move from Afterlife to Afterlife until we reach everlasting life. We realize that a cancer or a terminal illness cannot destroy our true selves because our true self is not our flesh, our mind, or our emotions. Our true self is our soul and our highest level of consciousness. Eternal bliss follows after our bodies are long gone. We realize that this enlightened part of our Universal Oneness can evolve and improve while we are alive if we spend time developing our spiritual growth.

How do we cultivate our Spiritual Oneness and spiritual growth? We must realize that nothing is missing in a perfect Spiritual Universe created by God. God has given us an abundance of all things and the know-how to find everything we need. Start to realize that there isn't any scarcity and become grateful for all that we have and all that is available to us. As the Bible says, "Ask and you shall receive." Grow your loving relationships with family and friends, thereby reducing separateness from those around you. Treat your pets lovingly and take walks enjoying all of nature. Remind yourself that "no man is an island" and that there is strength in numbers when it comes to the power of people, as the Bible tells us.

Do your best to have no enemies, unless they are trying to destroy your spirit or you are forced to defend your alignment with the whole of humanity. Meditate to increase your awareness of the meaning of life and your purpose for being here. You can use affirmations in your meditation such as:

"I love my life and my connection to Universal Oneness. I will allow only positive thoughts about other people to enter my mind."

"I will learn life's spiritual lessons, including being selfless instead of selfish, demonstrating humility, giving, and loving all of God's creatures."

"I will spread kindness and love instead of hatred and greed."

"I will spread the message of peace and avoid war."

Prayer

For those who prefer not to meditate, prayer may be your spiritual vehicle to connect with the Divine Universe or God and Universal Oneness. When you pray, try to avoid always asking God to do things for you. Instead, ask him to send signs to you for finding the righteous path. Tell God you love Him, that you will live with a strong faith in Him, and that you will follow his teachings. Tell God that you understand that your purpose in life is to become more Godlike. Pray for wellness and prosperity for all those you choose to pray for. Pray for man's destiny on Earth and for man's journey to reunite with God's love. Remember the "Golden Rule," in which Jesus states, "Do to others whatever you would like them to do to you" (Matt. 7.12a). Always put yourself in the other person's shoes. Remember when you see an addict or a homeless person on the street that, if it were not for God, that person could be you. Say a prayer for this person. Never make yourself more important than someone else, as part of your humility. We are all equals because we are all God's children.

"Love your neighbor as much as yourself." Visualize yourself as a Spirit on a spiritual journey. Try to see yourself as spiritual instead of being Caucasian, Hispanic, Asian, or Black. Imagine there are no borders to define countries and that we all live in one world. Recall or sing John Lennon's lyrics in the song *Imagine*:

> Imagine there's no countries
>
> It isn't hard to do
>
> Nothing to kill or die for
>
> And no religion too
>
> Imagine all the people
>
> Living life in peace
>
> You may say I'm a dreamer
>
> But I'm not the only one

I hope someday you'll join us

And the world will be as one

Imagine no possessions

I wonder if you can

No need for greed or hunger

A brotherhood of man

Imagine all the people

Sharing, all the world

You may say I am a dreamer

 But I'm not the only one

I hope someday you'll join us

And the world will live as one (Lennon)

We can live as One, and we can live in Universal Oneness.

Spiritual Oneness and the Afterlife

When we cross over to our Afterlife, eventually we will reunite with our parents, grandparents, and other relatives and friends. This may not occur immediately upon entering your first Afterlife, but it will happen at some point soon to follow. This tells us that Spiritual Oneness, which was very much an important part of our spiritual life in human form, continues after death. In this way, we are not only One with all living things, nature, the galaxies, and God, but we are also One with death and the Afterlife.

All things dead are always reborn. Cells in our bodies no longer needed are then destroyed by other parts of our bodies. The process of programmed cell death occurs in our bodies to eliminate unwanted cells. This process plays a role in preventing cancer. Red blood cells in our bodies can eliminate unwanted cells. Red blood cells live in our circulation 420 days before being engulfed by macrophages in the spleen, where they cease to exist. Afterwards, new red stem cells are born and developed in our bone marrow before entering our vascular circulation. Red blood cells are born and die continuously until our demise. Death and birth occur constantly and simultaneously in our bodies. Our bodies are no strangers to death; our physical forms are in the process of dying at all times. With each passing day, our organs function a little less well. The arteries in our body become a little more clogged as our hearts become slightly less efficient. In fact, all of our organ systems are slowly moving toward their inevitable termination.

Outside our bodies, we also see death everywhere. We see roadkill in the streets, flowers die, and people pass away. Currently, throughout the world, 120 people die every minute. Death is so much a part of life that we conclude that life and death are the same—they occur simultaneously. Like the death and rebirth of all living cells, as soon as our bodies die, we are reborn. Like Christ, we are resurrected as he promised to all those who believe in him. As we cross over into the new life, we once again are in Spiritual Oneness with ourselves, our families, our higher consciousness, and with the Universal Divine Energy or God. This is the Universal Oneness of the Afterlife. This time, we will be free from our physical form. Pain and suffering will no longer exist.

So then, why are most cultures and civilizations so fearful of death? We are fearful of death because we do not honestly believe that we are One at all times with those loved ones who have passed on. We also do not believe that we are One with Afterlife souls. Furthermore, though we may believe in a Divine Energy Source or God, we do not always feel Oneness with him while we are living. We are afraid that death is an end and not a beginning. Our faith is sometimes not strong enough to believe that death is rebirth.

If we so choose, our response to death can be a renewed promise to enjoy life on Earth. I believe the best view of death (a positive view) comes when we rely on our higher consciousness to bring us an enhanced perspective on death. We can utilize the spiritual tools of higher consciousness, meditation, and prayer, to faithfully affirm that our death is a celebration of new life in the next world, while also augmenting our love for our living time on Earth. By identifying with our Universal Oneness of life, death, and the Afterlife, we become less fearful of death, and our anxiety pertaining to our inevitable demise diminishes.

We should bond with our loved ones who have passed on. We should pray for them and speak with them often. Because the dead sometimes pass between worlds, they will very much hear you. While meditating or praying, think of your soul and higher consciousness fully enlightened in the Afterlife. Now connect and become One with your true self after you have crossed over. In time, you will become comfortable with who you are now and forever. Lastly, grow your relationship with Divine Energy or God (whichever term you are comfortable with). Meditate, pray, and talk to God more often. Form the strongest relationship with Divine Energy or God that you are capable of. Work on growing your relationship and belief in all aspects of Spiritual Oneness. Work on enhancing the spiritual virtues and spiritual lessons discussed in Chapter 2.

The wholeness or Universal Oneness of our souls' existence includes both life and death. Not including death and the Afterlife as part of our spiritual journey leaves humankind stuck in the limitations of our ego minds and our physical form. While life on Earth is imperfect, the spiritual movement of our soul from one life to the next is total perfection. Recognize Universal Oneness as physical, mental, emotional, and spiritual. Universal Oneness is the connection of all life, spirits, and nature on Earth, as well as all spirits and souls in the Afterlife.

Affirmation: "This morning, I bless the entire Universe of people, living animals, and things, so that we may all live in Spiritual Oneness."

CHAPTER 10
The Spirit of Intuition and Clairvoyance

Anyone with great imagination, of course, is intuitive. Knowledge of any nature, unless put into practical use, becomes of little effect.

—Edgar Cayce

Intuition in the Heavens

Splendid music is chirping above me, below me, and within me. I sense a euphonious melody coming both through the ears I no longer possess and also transmitting through bone conduction—unlike the experience of a person with a physical body. For a split second, I get fooled, thinking the hair on my arm is standing on end and small goosebumps line my extensor upper extremities. Of course, my arms are actually no longer physically present. The experience is like being on Earth and sensing a phantom arm after it's been amputated.

I awaken to the music but quickly realize I don't have a physical form. I really am suspended in time and space here in the Afterlife, as the celestial music penetrates all my soul. Colors are not as brilliant today as they usually are. As I begin to wonder why this might be, my consciousness intuitively picks up the answer almost immediately. I am too far from where bright colors might be.

I am predominantly located some one hundred billion lightyears from the Earth, which is about eighty-four billion lightyears farther then your most sophisticated stargazing telescope can see. Paradoxically, there are no discrete stars at this point in space. Similar to the way man thought that the Earth was flat, man thinks that outer space is populated with planets and stars continuing indefinitely. I have learned in the Afterlife that although space is infinite, it appears more as clouds of dust and distorted irregular shapes the farther you move away from the Milky Way.

My clairvoyant aptitude allows me to know my mother will be coming to see me today. It will be the first time I've met with her since I crossed over into my Afterlife. There are many spirits surrounding me now. Their white globes are bright, warm, and full of love, their essence embracing my total being as I feel exhilarated and blissful. Suddenly, Mom appears from both internal and external planes of existence. I know it is her because I feel protected and coddled in a way only she was capable of providing when I was a child. Although she has no physical form, I can feel her breath and sense the movement that can belong only to her. She has a specific frequency: this frequency radiates her special kindness, love, devotion, protection, and faith. It is an extremely fast, high frequency. Her spiritual virtues were already very well developed on Earth and are even better developed here in my Afterlife. My clairvoyance allows me to understand her spiritual evolution.

My mother and I were awfully close during my lifetime, but especially when I was in my twenties. On Sundays, we would often get in my car, and I would drive us from Long Island to Manhattan to attend Marble Collegiate Church, where we would listen to phenomenal Christian life messages expressed in the sermons of the great Norman Vincent Peale. At that time, my mom and I were both very spiritual and often discussed our spiritual beliefs. Mom would say, "If you believe in an Afterlife, Michael, there will be one waiting for you, and if you don't believe it, your body will just die, and that will be the end of you."

I didn't believe this and would say to her, "We all have souls, which continue after death." Of course, we both know now that I was right. All persons have souls that continue after death. Furthermore, all souls and all consciousness eventually reach the Kingdom of Heaven.

I told Mom that I had recently seen Dad. I told her that my discussion with him was very brief. I told her, "He was on his way to learn about Spiritual Oneness."

"Your dad could certainly use that spiritual lesson," she declared. We both laughed lightly. She repeated, "He certainly needs to learn that one." She told me that she had seen him not too long ago here in the Afterlife, but they really didn't have much to say to each other. I guess their lost love was still lost. I thought to myself, "Maybe things will be different in one of their other Afterlives." Our consciousness turned away from the subject of my dad. Mom let me know that she was so incredibly happy to be with me again. She continuously spread motherly love and understanding to me that intensified, making me feel richly empowered. She had made me feel this way on Earth as well.

My Mom was born in Denver, Colorado. She met my dad when he was in the military while stationed in Denver. She tells the story that they planned to get married and live in Denver. However, she says that after they were married, dad insisted they move back to his family in Queens, New York. She did so but claimed that moving to Queens made her very unhappy.

My dad's father (my grandfather) arrived on a boat from Italy when he was 11 years old. Although he was an avid reader of the newspaper, he never learned to write. The story is that he ruled the family with an iron fist. My grandfather and father believed that the man is the head of the household, and all were supposed to follow his rules. Mom says that my grandpa had a bad temper, and it was difficult for her and my father to live in the same apartment house with him.

Mom's life was vastly different from the life she had out west. Although we visited Mom's family in Denver many times, she was never able to move back home. This seemed to make her incredibly distraught. In time, Mom gave birth to two boys and two girls. I was the third child born. Although her children made her happy, my parents' marriage was fraught with anger and a lot of disagreements. Over the years, my mother had done the best she could to deal with my father's contentious personality.

My father didn't earn a lot of money, and this led to many arguments over family finances. My father would yell at my mother for spending too much money on groceries. He would also become angry with her for visiting neighborhood friends. In addition, my father had become dishonest regarding his relationships. After 37 years of marriage, they divorced.

My mother was always interested in spiritual life and metaphysical phenomena. There were times when she was paid to read astrological charts. She would use birth dates and time of birth from customers to describe details of their personalities. This information might steer a person toward a specific occupation. It would also tell the individual the type of personality of another person they were compatible with. Mom was also extremely interested in handwriting analysis and taught its principles and theories in Adult Education classes at many of the local schools.

Today, Mom and I discussed many of the events of our lives. We communicated by use of our telepathy and clairvoyance (much like talking without lip movement) about our experiences together and how we shared so many wonderful spiritual beliefs when we were alive. We shared how much we loved the sermons and books of the inspirational minister and spiritual author Norman Vincent Peale. Both my mom and I loved him dearly. We agreed that his positive thinking and spiritually uplifting messages were always the pinnacle of our Sunday church experiences.

My mother was so happy that I had successfully crossed over into my Afterlife. At this point, Mom gave me some motherly advice, saying, "Since you are the first of my children to cross over to the Afterlife, please go back to Earth and tell your siblings, their children, your children, and the grandchildren how important it is for them to live reverent lives. Tell them that their spiritual practices must supersede all matters of the flesh. Tell them to live by all of the spiritual virtues as often as possible. Let them know the importance of intuition in their lives. Tell them that intuition and clairvoyance can help them in both their current lives and their Afterlives. You may not be able to communicate with them when you first arrive in the living world. However, after some time, our Spirit selves are generally able to communicate with the living. If you are able to communicate with them, please tell them what I have advised and tell them how much I love them."

"I will absolutely do this," I said.

Then my mom said, "Michael, there is another thing I would like to discuss with you. I know that you think you lived your life in a selfish way. I want you to know that you are wrong. You sacrificed many years going out of your way to help sick patients. I also want to remind you that you were both a healer and a teacher. You taught many physician assistant students about medicine and helped launch their careers. Please don't forget that you mentored many of the medical residents. Although it was your profession, you often went the extra mile for them. Furthermore, I watched you closely with your children. You were a fantastic father and were extremely selfless when you were with them." Mom intuitively knew I was never certain I had been a good dad. I thanked my mom for all these compliments, which made me feel good about myself.

Mom felt certain that it would not take me long to reach the Kingdom of Heaven. I felt elated and emotionally fulfilled. She had always made me feel this way when we were alive, as well. She then said, "It is time for me to leave." She hoped that we would be able to see each other again, but neither of us was certain of this. She kissed me on the cheek, and she was gone. I was both sad and happy at the same time.

My clairvoyance told me it would be a while before I saw my mom and dad again. Despite this knowledge, it is wonderful how my intuition and clairvoyance are so available to me in the Afterlife. It allows Universal Knowledge and Universal Wisdom to permeate the essence of my being.

Intuition and Clairvoyance

Everyone has intuition. Being intuitive, similar to being psychic, uses energy that connects consciousness to everything that lies beyond our five senses. To become intuitive, one must clear their mind and reach new heights of awareness. Intuition is one of the main senses I call the *Spiritual Senses*.

The six Spiritual Senses consist of intuition, clairvoyance, insight, inspiration, awareness, and imagination. All of these Spiritual Senses become heightened by higher consciousness. During meditation, Spiritual Senses become poignant. They help us experience Spiritual Wisdom and insight into the Afterlife. These senses become well developed as we practice spiritual virtues with higher consciousness and awareness. As we learn our spiritual lessons, we use our Spiritual Senses as tools to escalate our spiritual growth in this world and as preparation for our Afterlife.

To develop intuition, one must be open to it and be passionate about learning. Information that comes to us can be received by our physical five senses (sight, taste, touch, smell, and hearing) or through our psychic Spiritual Senses of intuition or clairvoyance. Intuition can come to us visually, by hearing voices, by recognizing feelings, or by Universal Knowledge. All of us have intuition, but it is developed to different ability levels in each of us. Some people have exceedingly high intuition levels without even having practiced its development. We can think of these persons as "naturally intuitive." This can be immensely helpful if you read Tarot cards or practice fortune-telling, for instance. It can also be used in more useful ways, such as solving crimes or choosing a job. Intuition can alert us to danger and keep us safe.

Intuition can be useful but may not always be entirely accurate. These are times when your intuition is mostly based on a gut feeling. As the subconscious and conscious minds recognize prior thinking and prior outcomes based on knowledge acquired, the brain uses patterns based on prior experiences to make an educated guess, thereby making correct choices and decisions. However, intuition can paradoxically occur without prior patterns or learned mental knowledge. This is pure intuition rather than an educated guess because predictions are made without any prior knowledge.

If there are psychic phenomena occurring as part of the intuition process, such as a voice from a family member who is deceased, we may consider labeling the event as clairvoyant, since an ability beyond our five known physical senses is being utilized. Mediums who receive messages from dead entities utilize their clairvoyance. Mediums are able to use higher energy or vibrations to communicate with the Afterlife. Psychics use their 'sixth sense,' or psychic energy, to receive messages from the past, present, and future but do not usually communicate with spirits in the Afterlife. Although the terms 'psychic' and 'clairvoyant' are often used interchangeably, in its purest sense, a clairvoyant has a supernatural ability to perceive events in crystal-clear form and see crystal-clear images. Technically, clairvoyance is defined as 'clear seeing.' Clairaudience is known as 'clear hearing,' and clairsentience is 'clear feeling.' We can summarize clairvoyance by saying it is the claimed ability to gain information about an object, person, or physical event through extrasensory perception.

In general, the meaning of intuition is not as specific or as sophisticated as the terms psychic or clairvoyant. For our discussion, intuition is discerning something that one knows or considers likely without the need for conscious reasoning or previous knowledge. When we speak about intuition relating to death or the Afterlife, we may use the more paranormal term, clairvoyant.

What are some examples of intuition? How can intuition help you in your life? When you are called into the boss's office, you may start to wonder, "What will he tell or ask me?" If your intuition tells you, "This will be really bad," you may ask your manager to come into the office with you. The manager may clarify a problem the boss thought you created, thereby reducing the boss's anger. By having the intuition to bring the manager with you, you may avoid being fired.

The baseball coach is about to start his strongest pitcher (who has the most wins), but he gets a "hunch" or has intuition that his second-string pitcher will perform better that day. He sends the second-string pitcher into the game. The coach who starts his second-string pitcher at the last minute may go on to win the baseball game.

When we are certain someone is about to say something before they say it, with no prior knowledge, once again, it is our gut-feeling or internal intuitive consciousness at work. If we already know what someone is about to say, we can prepare our appropriate response in advance or have available the information they are about to ask us for.

Intuition allows us to prepare information, find a solution to a problem, avoid danger, make money, and avoid illness. These are just a few positive ways we can utilize intuition.

Charity, on a first date, thinks the guy she meets seems nice enough, but she senses via intuition that there is something very wrong with him and avoids a second date. A month later, she finds out he is being accused of raping a woman on a second date. Charity's intuition helps her avoid the dangerous rapist.

Faith develops a slight pain in her left breast. She has a history of fibrocystic disease, and after her doctor's examination of her left breast, the doctor attributes the discomfort to inflammatory cysts and sends her home. After a few days, the pain in her left breast is about the same, but her intuition is telling her something is very wrong! She returns to the doctor and demands that an ultrasound or CAT scan be performed. The doctor agrees to diagnostic testing. After testing, it is found that a biopsy is necessary. You guessed it—Faith has breast cancer. In this case, Faith's own intuition concerning her health became dramatically important. In essence, Faith saved her own life. As a side note, you are always your own best health advocate.

If we agree that intuition is real, that it is helpful, and that the quality and amounts of intuition vary in folks, how can we further develop our intuition? We start by trying to predict outcomes. Whenever you are about to do something important, try to visualize and hear the future occurrence playing out. Allowing yourself to feel your emotions in advance will be helpful in discerning the desired outcome. This is the same way that we fully use intention and the Law of Attraction. We visualize and hear the desired outcome before it takes place, and we enjoy the feelings of reaching the goal as though we have already attained it.

Clear your mind, stay calm, and allow your awareness to magnify, the same way one does while meditating. Be as insightful as you can by assimilating prior knowledge of people, places, and events that are the same or similar to the events that are about to take place. Always keep a positive attitude about how future occurrences will come to pass—know the ramifications will be wonderful. Have faith that your intuition is on point, and believe in yourself. Incredible results will follow. Practice being intuitive as much as possible, as "practice makes perfect." Pay attention to your dreams while sleeping. Your subconscious mind is continually working on creating solutions to the questions you have asked yourself during the day. Augment your creativity by painting, reading, drawing, writing, or listening to music. A free, creative mind will help open the doors to intuition.

Listen to your 'inner thermostat.' Your inner thermostat (which originates in the hypothalamus) is your physical body's regulator of cold and warm temperatures when it must react to the environment. Your hypothalamus can also react similarly to problems or events. Feelings, sensations, and awareness of your body's thermostatic reactions will guide your intuition in a general way toward "go versus stop" and "positive versus negative." When you think of something about to transpire, do you get an unrestful cold feeling in your gut, or a warm feeling in your central chest and shoulders? Becoming aware of these bodily temperature sensations will help you to make good intuitive decisions.

Align yourself with the virtues of love, kindness, faith, charity, beauty, honesty, courage, compassion, and perseverance to better sense clear intuition. Further, align your true self with the Spiritual Senses of intuition, clairvoyance, insight, inspiration, awareness, and imagination. Meditate daily, if possible. Meditation calms your mind, opens you to supernatural ideas, and augments your awareness of true reality beyond the five physical senses. Permit intuition and clairvoyance to become actively part of your character. Pray often that you will use your intuition in righteous ways. Pray on solving problems utilizing intuition. Prayer can give you the power to see multiple solutions and righteous spiritual paths. Prayer uses intuition to open up our being, both internally (physically) and externally (spiritually), to see all the infinite possibilities, thus creating an all-encompassing mundane and Universal Knowledge, resulting in perfect solutions. In the cosmic or metaphysical world, as well as in the spiritual world, intuition exists in all insightful and imaginative souls.

As a person in the Afterlife, I look back at my previous existence on Earth and realize that I had limited intuition and sometimes missed chances to enhance my intuitive possibilities. I don't want this to happen to you. For example, when I was choosing a college to attend, I picked Hofstra University because it was close to my family home. I was familiar with Long Island, New York, so I felt safe. They offered psychology (which I was interested in), and I had a choice to commute or live in the dormitories. However, I didn't pay attention to my intuition, which was telling me not to enroll. When I visited the campus, my internal thermostat told me it was cold and somewhat unfriendly. The school was also overly expensive, and my funds were limited. Later, I knew my intuition had been right when I felt that the University did not fit me. Many students had a haughty air about them, the professors were rigid, and the atmosphere was cold in general. I often wished I had listened to my intuition.

During several of my employments during my forty-year medical career as a physician assistant, I stayed at some specific employments too long. I remained for too long in cardiovascular surgery and also with my employers in plastic and reconstructive surgery. Leaving those positions more quickly would have allowed me to gather a more in-depth, comprehensive understanding of medicine and exposed me to more vital patient care. I would have also received greater financial remuneration. I wish I had followed my intuition and left these employment positions sooner than I did.

Intuition and Clairvoyance in the Afterlife

After the transformation to my Afterlife, I sometimes move between the two worlds of the living and the dead. The more I do this, the more I learn that intuition and clairvoyance are much more part of the Afterlife than the living world. Intuition, and even more so, clairvoyance, is an elevated level of consciousness that mainly takes place frequently and with accuracy in the Afterworld. Telepathy is usually described as mind-reading or defined as 'the communication of thoughts and ideas by means other than the five known senses.' Telepathy, pure intentions, and clairvoyance happen more often in the Afterlife than in the living world. Here in the Afterlife, clairvoyance and telepathy have almost no limitations. This is because all the spirits in the Afterlife are One with themselves, each other, and the Divine Universe.

As we move toward true spiritual reality in the Afterlife, most individuality is lost as we all become more Godlike. After we experience many Afterlives and reach true Enlightenment, often called the Kingdom of Heaven, individuality is completely shed.

Think back on the intuitive events of your life. If comfortable with meditation or prayer, use these tools to visualize yourself dead and reflect on the events of your intuitive and clairvoyant life. How intuitive are you? Is your intuition better now, or was it better when you were younger? How has intuition helped you in your life events? Do you believe intuition can involve a spiritual energy that exceeds your physical five senses? Do you want to further develop your intuition and clairvoyance? What steps will you take to improve your intuitive and clairvoyant aptitudes? One of your goals in life should be to develop your intuition, as it is a big part of your spiritual evolution. It is one of the spiritual lessons we are put on Earth to learn. If you develop a keen sense of intuition in life, it will not only greatly help you succeed in this world but will also carry over to your spiritual Afterlife. Intuition is a major component of the soul. Tapping into our soul's energy as soon as possible will help lift our spiritual lives now and eternally. Utilizing your imaginary death allows you to understand intuition's spiritual role in your life and learn a better way to live.

Affirmation: "I can develop my intuition by practicing the prediction of outcomes and events before they happen."

Live Like You Are Dying

CHAPTER 11
Health and Supreme Spiritual Health

Health is a state of complete harmony of the body, mind, and
spirit. When one is free from physical disabilities and mental
distractions, the gates of the soul open.

—B.K.S. Iyengar

Health in My Afterlife

You are probably wondering how we can discuss health in a world with entities who don't have physical bodies. The answer is shockingly simple. In the Afterlife, there is spiritual health without corporeal form. There is spiritual health and Supreme Spiritual Health. Spiritual health has an extremely broad and comprehensive meaning.

The meaning and significance of spiritual health in the Afterlife involves improving on our spiritual lessons learned. As we become more virtuous and righteous, our spiritual health becomes better and better. This improvement in spiritual health leads us to Supreme Spiritual Health. To fully understand this concept of Supreme Spiritual Health, we must distinguish between good health and supremely good health. On Earth, it would be the difference between feeling well and feeling invigorated and full of energy. Supreme Spiritual Health may require multiple successive Afterlives to feel the full health benefit.

Before we can further delve into the concept of Supreme Spiritual Health, we must introduce a particularly important concept regarding health in my Afterlife and all Afterlives in general. The concept is that entities without a physical form can still experience physical pleasures in the Afterlife. For instance, where I currently live, I do not need a nervous system to experience the joy of the great sensations of massage. Similarly, without a physical body, I still get extreme pleasure from experiencing my favorite music. In the Afterlife, all wonderful emotions can still be experienced even though I am without physical form. I can still feel the gratification of achievement, the elation of winning the *Readers Digest Sweepstakes*, the joyous laughter of being tickled, the zest of winning my first tennis tournament, and the contentment of delicious food filling my belly, all despite not having physical form. With this understanding that a physical form is not necessary to experience the greatest of worldly pleasures, let's return to our discussion of Supreme Spiritual Health.

I attain Supreme Spiritual Health in my Afterlife when all feelings of joy, pleasure, and satisfaction become seven times as enjoyable as they were on Earth. This also applies to enjoyment experienced in feelings of security, safety, confidence, kindness, love, and more. The kind of positive feelings experienced sevenfold is only curtailed by my imagination. With all these amplified sensations of bliss, it is now impossible to feel spiritually unhealthy. I become more than spiritually healthy; I become Supremely Spiritually Healthy. Whereas you are spiritually healthy while still having spiritual lessons and spiritual virtues to learn, Supreme Spiritual Health implies that that there are very few, if any, spiritual lessons left to learn or spiritual virtues to act upon.

With my physical form gone, I feel positive sensations in my mind, heart, and gut magnified seven-fold. I experience the elation of a "runner's high" multiplied by at least seven. I experience tender love, both personal and Universal, that is far greater than I experienced on Earth. The pleasure I previously felt in my gut when my son graduated college is heightened sevenfold. This is all part of Supreme Spiritual Health.

Some of you who die may initially be unhappy without physical form because you cannot workout in the gym for one hour, five days a week. You may feel sadly nostalgic that you will not be going sailing or mountain climbing anymore. Do not fret, as all these physical activities still produce joyous feelings even if you are not physically doing them. Much like virtual reality in the Metaverse, you will experience all these activities without being there—although you will not need the headset. The same wonderful sensations will continue to be elicited and received in the Afterlife. Only this time, they will be enjoyed multiple times over. We do not need physical form when we have higher consciousness to attain these wonderful feelings and sensations. The realm of higher consciousness creates a special spiritual awareness or realization that allows for all pleasures to be magnified beyond our wildest dreams. Supreme Spiritual Health and happiness are unavoidable when my higher consciousness allows me to live in a multi-factorial (sevenfold) state of bliss. As this happens, I actualize Supreme Spiritual Health.

With each passing Afterlife, the memory of my physical form on Earth is progressively lost. With the passage of time (which, of course, does not exist), I no longer remember the pleasure that my physical form made possible. I no longer remember to what degree I experienced joy when I shot my lowest golf score. I no longer remember the amount of accomplishment I felt when I received my first huge raise at work. With that memory gone, there are no comparisons to be made. I only know that all these feelings are magnified in my Afterlife. With no direct comparisons, sadness is not possible. I no longer compare my healthy state of joy in the Afterlife with health or illness on Earth. My low standard for physical and spiritual health on Earth is forgotten and replaced with 700% Supreme Spiritual Health in the Afterlife. My energy is essentially limitless now. We can feel healthy energy with or without a physical body. My positive feelings of vitality, vigor, and strength are unimaginably robust in my Afterlife

I am no longer limited by the five senses of sight, taste, hearing, smell, and touch. In my Afterlife, my Spiritual Senses of intuition, clairvoyance, imagination, insight, awareness, and inspiration are seven times greater than on Earth. In my Afterlife, I now experience multiple additional senses beyond the six Spiritual Senses; unfortunately, these new senses are impossible to describe in words.

I am no longer limited to the four dimensions of length, width, depth, and time. *String Theory,* a modern physics model, is correct in theorizing that there are ten-plus dimensions (Berman). New experiences of thriving with numerous senses in multi-dimensions make my Afterlife exhilarating and knowledge-provoking, resulting in my spiritual omnipotence. These additional senses and dimensions in my current state of higher consciousness all contribute to my Supreme Spiritual Health.

With enlightened righteousness, my physical and emotional pleasures immensely magnified, and physical health and illness on Earth forgotten, my Supreme Spiritual Health reigns vitally dominant in my Afterlife. Experiencing ten-plus dimensions in the Afterlife, I have a better understanding of the Spiritual Universe, and positive Universal Energy keeps me in excellent health.

Let's return to the non-fiction part of the book now and discuss health on Earth. I warn you that it may be a little less stimulating than these last few pages. However, the anecdote is necessary to explain the important role that health plays in your life.

Health on Earth

I worked as a physician assistant for approximately forty years. I worked seven years in cardiothoracic surgery, nineteen years in plastic and reconstructive surgery, and fourteen years in dermatology. I started my medical career at twenty-four years old in 1981 in New York City and retired from medicine at age sixty-six in Connecticut. Through those years of collaborating with physicians and patients in hospitals and private practices, I learned much about the process of human aging. There is a branch of medicine called geriatrics, and the medical noun for the state of being old is known as senescence.

One of my patients once asked me, "Have you heard of old age being known as the golden years?"

I said, "Yes, of course."

He said, "Well, they aren't so golden!"

My patient, of course, was referring to the many physical disabilities and illnesses related to aging. The aged commonly develop infirmities such as high blood pressure, diabetes, heart disease, thyroid disease, arthritis, cancers, hearing loss, cataracts, obesity, hemorrhoids, and many more. I would bore and upset you if I continued to list all the common illnesses the aged experience. Imagine if I also listed all the less-common conditions.

Most people who are middle-aged or older are aware that the elderly take a lot of medication for their diseases. What most younger adults and middle-aged adults don't realize is that many adults in their 50s, 60s, and 70s begin to have simultaneous multiple organ system disease. For instance, it is common to develop arthritis, prostate disease, and high cholesterol all within a three-to-five-year period. They sometimes don't appreciate that the greater the number of diseases a person develops, the more this may affect his quality of life.

As the elderly person (or patient) develops more disease, several medications are required. A person with diabetes, for instance, may need to take two to three medications for just that one condition. Those with five to six diagnoses may require seven to fifteen medications per day. In addition, each medication may have to be taken two to three times per day. Keep in mind, these numbers are not atypical. Some of these medications may be oral, and some may require self-injection or suppositories. Some treatments may require the patient to go to an infusion center. Besides the cost of all these medications, keeping track of taking them at the scheduled times sometimes becomes a difficult task. The specifics regarding refills, pick-up, and doctors' orders, as well as learning the side effects of each medication, can be very challenging. Attention must also be given to drug interactions and abstinence from alcohol.

Most of the time, the elderly in America are on small, fixed budgets. The financial strife, along with physical ailments, can make their lives a great challenge. In recent years, the isolation caused by the coronavirus and its variants have caused growing numbers of our elderly population anxiety and depression.

Why am I going into all this detail about health on Earth? Remember that we all are a combination of our physical (mortal), fleeting selves and our divine, spiritual, eternal selves. It is extremely important for all of us to realize we are spiritually enlightened entities living in physical bodies. We are not physical bodies who happen to have a spiritual side within us. Our body is only a physical form or shell. It is not who we truly are. Our true identity is our Spirit. Each of us is a thoughtful, emotional, and spiritual entity with a divine soul that will never perish. However, if we do not take care of our physical bodies and they cease to exist, then how can we grow spiritually on Earth? We cannot. We must approach total wellness and health with an interest in our spiritual health, mental health, and physical health on Earth. Our physical bodies, mental states, and spiritual selves must all remain healthy for us to remain happy and free of illness and stress.

Our physical bodies won't last. As we age, our physical bodies break down like an old car. Certain parts can sometimes be fixed or replaced, but eventually, the car is not drivable anymore. Stop putting so much emphasis on physical form and start reaching for your divine, true self. Your true self, also called your authentic self, is your soul at its purest. Bring your soul to life now by connecting with your higher consciousness and the spiritual power of Universal Energy. You may suddenly see your physical health improve when you have this mindset. Our spiritual self will go on eternally. Our true self, which is our spiritual self, never dies. The problem occurs when we emphasize our physical bodies much more than our connection to our Divine Energy Source or God because, with that misdirected focus, we will never learn the best way to live. When we reach senescence, we will only know how to concentrate on our aches, pains, and sufferings because we did not sufficiently experience the power of God throughout our entire life. We did not spend sufficient time connecting with God through conversation, prayer, and meditation. One of the main purposes for living is to learn the spiritual lesson that we will never die (even though death appears to look so final). A second purpose for living is to learn that God's power is working in our lives all the time. We must learn this spiritual lesson regarding health. Our approach to health must be holistic. Health includes soundness of body, mind, and spirit. We must treat all these components of health with serious attention and awareness.

Do you think the eighteen-year-old shooter in Uvalde, Texas, would have killed nineteen children and two teachers if he had developed his spiritual self and had a strong spiritual faith or connection with God? Of course not. There are many reasons that mass murder (killing four persons or more at one time) events have been increasing across our country. Many of these are related to gun laws, lack of school security, and mental illness. There is, however, another incredibly significant reason for these mass killings that many people overlook. Most young people have not been raised with a spiritual education and have little or no relationship with Divine Energy or God. If we could get younger people to understand that their true self is their righteous spirit and reverent soul, mass killings would diminish. When people of any age practice spiritual virtues and have good moral values, violence and killing are not part of their thoughts and intentions. The result is we all stay safe. We must keep our children and all citizens of the United States safe. Regarding children, in the Gospel of Luke, Jesus says, "Let the little children come to me. Don't stop them! For the Kingdom of God belongs to those who are like these children. I tell you the truth, anyone who doesn't receive the Kingdom of God like a child will never enter it" (Luke 18.16-17b).

After working in the medical field for such a long time, I have some takeaways. Let me share a few with you. Firstly, modern medicine is extremely limited in many ways. There are many illnesses that do not have any treatments at all. Think about how difficult it is just to treat the common cold. In this day of coronavirus, we have all realized that we are highly vulnerable to viruses that are with us now and that will be with us in the future. It seems that endemic and pandemic diseases are becoming a part of our everyday life. Although we are starting to find vaccines and treatments for these viruses, we realize that these too have limitations. It becomes exceedingly difficult to treat viruses when they mutate rapidly into new variants. Think about arthritis, which is one of the most common joint diseases that people suffer from, if they live long enough. Arthritis has no cure. Treatments like nonsteroidal anti-inflammatories have adverse effects that sometimes lead to conditions worse than the arthritis itself. If taken too often, nonsteroidal anti-inflammatory medications can result in damage to your stomach and heart. I used to half-joke by saying, "Antibiotics have been the only breakthrough in modern medicine in the last one-hundred years. Now they don't want us to take antibiotics because this creates antibiotic resistance."

Doctors are limited by a lack of medical and scientific knowledge of the times. Many of them do not use their higher consciousness and have trouble utilizing the power of Universal Knowledge and Universal Wisdom. To only be book smart is not enough. For this reason, you must become your own best health advocate. No one is more concerned about your health than you are. You can help yourself by researching your own illnesses and medical conditions and getting more than one professional opinion. You can also seek alternative medicines.

My second takeaway is to be in tune with your body, mind, and spirit. You know your own body better than anyone else. You know substances that you are sensitive to, such as medications that you should not take, foods that make you feel better, and foods that make you feel worse. You know when your body has done too much exercise and when your body has not exercised enough. You can feel it when your body is run-down and tired. You know if you are slightly sick or extremely ill before anyone else does. Listen to the messages that your body, mind, and spirit are sending you; they almost always know what you need. Use your intuition to make your own diagnosis before you go to see the doctor. Become intuitive regarding treatments and remedies. Your gut feeling or intuition will tell you when something is not right with your body and your mind.

My third takeaway is for you to always check for drug interactions between the medications you are taking. When prescribed a new medication, ask the pharmacist if the new medication can interact with your current medications. You can also check for medication interactions by using a drug interaction site online. These web sites are usually free and easy to use.

The next point is that the body can often repair itself. Usually, when you get over a cold or a virus, it is because your body's immune system has destroyed the infection, and the medication that you took was only palliative—that is, it makes you feel better. The medication treats the symptoms but is often not doing anything to *cure* the illness.

Small bones may repair themselves. Often, if you break a toe, the healthcare professional will just have you tape it or splint it because he knows that the body will repair the fracture itself. Even certain cancers are held in check by the body's own defense mechanisms. While working in dermatology, I personally witnessed squamous cell skin cancers go away on their own. Whenever your body has a chance of healing itself without treatment, give it the chance to do so because then you will not have to concern yourself with the adverse effects of the medication. You will also not have to deal with potential, unintended mistakes made by the practitioner.

Realize that the physical body, mind, and spirit work in unison. The patient who is very depressed or has another extreme mental disorder will frequently also have persistent physical complaints that may be excessive. The patient will then become very anxious about the physical symptoms they are experiencing. This is known as somatic symptom disorder, when a cycle of physical pain and mental anguish occurs and reoccurs. Sometimes the same patient will believe routine medical examinations and diagnostic testing are life-threatening. A person with somatic symptom disorder is not faking their physical symptoms; they may or may not have discovered a legitimate medical problem. It is the patient's extreme reaction and behaviors associated with the physical symptoms that become the main issue. The field of somatic psychotherapy was developed to try to treat patients with this disorder, as well as other diseases. Somatic psychotherapy is a holistic approach that includes treatment of a person's body, mind, spirit, and emotions. It recognizes that attitudes, emotions, and beliefs can all affect a person's physical health. Often, past traumas may be related to somatic symptom disorder. Treatments may include cognitive behavior therapy, mindfulness-based therapy, pharmacotherapy, and St. John's wort (Likurlansik et al. 49-54A). In summary, the body, mind, and spirit can work either in harmony or in opposition to one another when it comes to mental and physical health.

My last takeaway regarding health is for you to recognize the importance of your spiritual well-being and use your spiritual energy to destroy disease and maintain good health. The Divine Energy Source or God will give you access to Universal Wisdom. This wisdom includes the knowledge and understanding of medical illness and effective treatments. In matters pertaining to disease and your health, collaborate with Divine Energy and God when you contemplate the issues of your illness, treatments, and especially your prognosis. The use of meditation and prayer will be most helpful.

When it comes to illness, there are always choices that will have to be made. We learn that there are diverse options when choosing treatment paths. As we get older and our health begins to fail, we are faced with many decisions. Will you want conservative treatment or aggressive treatment? Every individual gets to decide and agree to the plan of treatment he desires. Remember that a physician is only making his or her best recommendations, but it is up to you to decide what is in your best interest. In essence, you as the patient have the final say regarding your treatment.

Ask the Divine Energy Source or God to stay with you during any difficult health events or medical decision-making. Ask God to give you the power to understand the illness and all its ramifications. You may ask God through meditation or prayer to make the right choices to have a successful outcome. Even though these times are particularly challenging, spread spiritual virtues to all the professionals that you will be interacting with. People like kindness, honesty, integrity, and all niceties shed in their direction. God will be happy to see you overcome adversity and is most likely to empower you with an acceptance of all the medical challenges you will face.

When your body repairs itself, it will be one of your most glorious days, and you will live happily for many years to come. If, however, your disease becomes chronic and fatal, allow yourself to embrace your spiritual higher consciousness and affirm that the Afterlife will be your wonderful rebirth, knowing in your heart that you will be free from all pain and suffering for eternity. Come to the realization that by leaving your physical form, your spiritual self will transcend all strife experienced in this world. Your Afterlife will be the start of a new spiritual journey where you will learn any remaining spiritual lessons not learned on Earth. Once the spiritual lessons are learned in your Afterlives, you will be ready to have eternal bliss in the Kingdom of Heaven.

Pain Management

At the end of the Hulu TV series *Dopesick*, Michael Keaton closes the last episode with the following statement about pain:

"There's some kind of pain and, a lot of us, all of us, that we just don't want to feel anymore. The further we fall into addiction, and pain says to us: Hell, I'd be better off just feeling nothing at all. Until we go numb, and our souls go numb. Now, we got a real problem. You know, pain is just pain—not good, not bad, just part of being a human being. And sometimes good can come out of it, if we're brave enough and willing to go a little deeper—work our way through it, try to overcome it—well, we just might find our better selves" (Strong).

While I don't agree that pain is good, I do believe it is part of the human condition. I also agree with Keaton's point that if we work hard at getting rid of pain, we may overcome it. At some point in life, we all live with pain. Hopefully, it will just be for short periods of time, but for many, pain can become chronic. For this reason, there is now a medical specialty in the field of medicine known as pain management. The doctors and other providers who work in pain management have many tools at their disposal to help people get through pain. Some of these are steroid injections, Transcutaneous Electrical Nerve Stimulation (TENS), physical therapy, epidural injections, sympathetic nerve blocks, massage therapy, radiofrequency ablation, surgery, medication, biofeedback, exercise, acupuncture, chiropractic adjustments, and many others. Nobody should have to live with pain day in and day out. Pain that persists over a long period of time can cause deep depression. It is important that those in pain seek medical treatment immediately. If a particular treatment is not working, then try another one. The most important thing is to not give up. We must maintain good mental health. Do your best through meditation and prayer to find a solution to ending your pain. If one doctor or facility is not able to help you within a reasonable and acceptable timeframe, then seek care elsewhere. If at any point during treatment you feel that you may be dependent on or addicted to pain medication, immediately express your concerns to your healthcare providers. In the long run, opioid addiction will do more harm than the initial pain. Opioids should only be given for a short, monitored period of time, and your healthcare professionals should keep a close watch on this.

Good Nutrition and Exercise

Exercise daily and eat healthy foods. Exercise your body, mind, and spirit. To exercise your body, perform some kind of aerobic exercise forty-five minutes to one hour per day. This will keep your muscles toned, your organs vital, and help to keep your weight down. Exercise your mind by reading, writing, playing games, and engaging in good conversation. Exercise your spirit through prayer and meditation. Speak with Divine Energy or God on a regular basis.

To eat healthy, make sure you consume the required, but not excessive, calories and eat all the food groups, including proteins, carbohydrates, and lipids. Keep proportions appropriate so that weight gain will be minimized. Eat whole grains, lots of fruits and vegetables, and organic foods when appropriate. Make sure you are getting enough vitamins and minerals by meeting the standard *recommended daily allowances.*

Putting Your House in Order

Before closing, let's discuss "putting your house in order" before your transformation to your Afterlife. As adults, we should create a "Last Will and Testament." Do this as soon as possible. Do not assume that you have many years ahead of you to complete this task. Since death can come at any age, our monetary holdings and our possessions should be directed to those we choose (usually our children). If you do not create a Will prior to your death, your assets will go into probate and the state will have control of distribution in accordance with state law instead of your wishes. In certain situations, starting to distribute your assets to your children prior to your demise may make a lot of sense. Sometimes children may need the money now more than later, plus you will get to enjoy the spiritual virtue of giving.

The Advance Healthcare Directive, also known as the *Living Will,* is a document you should also consider creating prior to your demise. The Advance Healthcare Directive is a medical decision you make prior to your death that specifies your preferences regarding doctors' and caregivers' actions in the event you become terminally ill, enter a coma, or develop dementia, for instance (Mayo Clinic Staff).

A healthcare proxy, also known as a power of attorney, names the person you choose to act as your healthcare agent. This proxy is used when your physical or mental state requires someone to make medical decisions and judgments for you. A power of attorney grants someone the authority to act temporarily or permanently on behalf of another person in specified legal or financial matters ("Power of Attorney"). You should consider creating a document that names your power of attorney. A power of attorney can be utilized while you are alive and after you die.

A Durable Power of Attorney is different from a Power of Attorney in that it remains in effect even if the grantor becomes incapacitated and unable to make decisions for themselves. There are Durable Power of Attorney documents for managing financial affairs and for matters related to healthcare or medical decisions.

Conclusion

The subject of health is complex. Much further detail on the subject of health would be beyond the scope of this book. What I would like you to take away from this chapter is that good health in this world can be here today but very quickly gone tomorrow. Each of us must take care of our body, mind, and spiritual self, and not depend on anyone to do this for us. Exercise, eat right, keep your mind active, and see your internist on a routine basis. Be your own health advocate and do not be afraid to tell your doctor all of your concerns. Pray to the Divine Energy Source or God that you will have good health. Come to terms with the fact that, at some point, your health will fail. When that happens, your spirituality will help you live through this challenging time. Try to develop your spiritual self many years before your good health leaves you. Feel comfort in knowing that when you cross over into your new life, you will be free of pain and suffering forever. Use your spiritual insight to figure out how to deal with your current disease. Controlling your mind and your spiritual self will help you deal with your physical ailments. Always be grateful for the time you were gifted good health by Divine Energy. It is my sincere hope that by reading about my Afterlife earlier in this chapter, you can understand how insight and intuition can keep you mentally, physically, and spiritually healthy. When you live a righteous life, you create Supreme Spiritual Health. Someday you will shed your physical form, and you will experience true health that is greater than you could have ever imagined.

Affirmation: "I have supreme health and feel completely energized and invigorated."

CHAPTER 12
Love and Spiritual Love

Three things will last forever—faith, hope, and love—and the greatest of these is love.

—1 Corinthians 13:13

Love in the Afterlife

Heaven opened up as the beautiful colored gases of the atmosphere separated. High above me and in front of my being, where my head used to be, there appeared only an impression of two Earthly, gigantic, cerulean-blue eyeballs. Perfectly colored and diamond-shaped, the three-foot floating eyes generated a colossal force of love that enveloped my total spiritual being. At the same time, a brilliant, glorious light shined down on me from the same source. There was no question that this was God! The love I felt was more powerful than the culmination of all the love I had ever experienced while alive on Earth. It was a bounty of love that had no beginning and no end. God began to speak to me. Telepathically, he bellowed, "Michael, bring love to each waking day of life. Wake up to love by giving thanks to the glorious day before you. Say to yourself and to me, "This is the day the Lord hath made; let us rejoice and be glad in it." Turn to your loved one, pull her into your bosom, and tell her you love her. Hug each child when you see them so they can feel your love radiate from your spiritual core into their souls." Suddenly, God created images of moments from my prior life on Earth. I could see my twenty-eight-year-old mother cradling me in the old, gold rocking chair in our living room in Queens, New York. I could now feel the same emotions and thoughts of love that I experienced when I was a child. Her love oozed forth comforting feelings of safety, security, serenity, trust, and protection.

The next image God displayed was on the biggest high-definition TV monitor I had ever seen. It was five-dimensional, and the images came in waves. I was eight years old, and I was reliving a homerun I hit when I was in Little League. I felt the wonderful Louisville Slugger wood-grain bat in the palms of my calloused hands as I took a mighty swing and hit the baseball between the left and right outfielders. As I rounded the bases, I smelled the aroma of the sweet grass enter my nostrils and felt the smooth, reddish-orange beam clay of the infield under my thin sneakers. Home run! I was practically in tears. I was so *in love* with baseball at that moment. I could feel my heart race and goosebumps erupt on my skin. I was totally exhilarated when I jumped on home plate. My teammates greeted me by pushing their little hands and bodies against mine.

Next, God created colorful pictures of the beautiful young women that were most dear to me in my prior life. He allowed me a glimpse of the love I shared with each of them when our love was at its peak. I had forgotten so much. I realized that my life had been filled with so much genuine love. I felt so blessed and wished I had appreciated all their love more when I was alive. God showed me images of all my marriages, each special in their own way. The weddings included the gowns, the cakes, the people who attended, and the photographs. All were amazing, but the powerful emotion of love for each and every one of them was somehow everlasting. None of that love would ever be removed, as it was immortalized in heaven. For those of you who have been in love and have lost that love, feel hopeful in knowing that love is eternal. The end of that love is an illusion. It continues within the Divine Universe.

God displayed in my Afterlife my final love relationship with Kathy. Because our special love for each other was the most powerful and most recent, it penetrated feelings of bliss deep within my spiritual soul. My love for her made me feel totally connected to the Universe and helped inspire the writing of this chapter.

As the pictures of these women faded, God revealed my first son, Adam, being born. I recall that I wasn't sure about wanting any children. My father's frequent anger and abuse of all our family made me afraid to be a dad. Here I was, seeing myself in the delivery room on my way to becoming a father. I was between my wife's stirrups and the heavy blue surgical drapes in the delivery room. My wife was having difficulty pushing Adam out of her vaginal canal. The obstetrician took this huge suction device and placed it over the crown of Adam's skull. The machine and doctor vacuumed and pulled three times until Adam was born. The suction machine made the crown of his skull into a cone shape. Suddenly, true love poured from my heart! From the depths of my soul, a cascade of exuberant love emanated from me toward my newborn baby, my wife, and all the doctors and nurses in the room. It was a spiritual miracle. I was a dad. At that moment, I knew that there was nothing better in life than the love I felt for that baby, my wife, and for life itself. As I thought about how incredible love in the world was, God granted me beautiful images of my second son, Joseph, who I also watched being born. I was feeling the entire love experience all over again, three years later. He, too, was suctioned out and had the beautiful little cone-shaped occipital skull for several weeks, just like his brother. I just adored and loved everything about him. Joseph was a lanky little infant boy who, like his brother, would grow to become an amazing spiritual man at the time of this writing. The word Joseph means "to add on," and he was certainly a Godlike addition to our family.

God wasn't finished with me. As I was beginning to feel a little emotionally depleted, God began to bellow out principles of love to me: "Michael, love is the Universal antidote for all of life's challenges and strife. Where there is love, there will be no violence, fear, anger, jealousy, condemnation, lust, or guilt. When there is love, the other spiritual virtues will follow. These are faith, hope, charity, kindness, fortitude, prudence, humility, temperance, patience, diligence, justice, honesty (truth), awareness, and perseverance. It is love that makes all the preceding virtues possible. Love is who I am and who you are. Love is in all the people of the world, but it lays dormant much of their lives. When people make love their spiritual priority, the vices and sins melt and diminish in perpetuity."

God continued, "Please share your love with me. Talk to me every day. It is especially important to talk to me when you need help with life's challenges, disappointments, and divisiveness. There are evil moments in life that are beyond the human being's ability to confront on his own. During those times, let go and let me take over. You cannot always do it yourself. I will bring you the peace and calm you need when it is otherwise impossible. Realize that all the love you have experienced in your lifetime has come from me. Give thanks and praise to me, and we will reunite at the time of death. Michael, tell the people of the world that at the hour of their death, they should look to the heavens and seek my cerulean blue eyes parting the heavens and creating the spiritual light. At that hour, all persons will be comfortable as they look to me and their loved ones to reunite in a blissful love that lasts eternally. Michael, return to Earth now and speak of love." I was totally shaken but answered his command by returning to Earth to write the rest of this chapter.

Spiritual Love and Relationships

There are an infinite number of ways to approach the subject of love because, through the centuries, there have been millions of mindful statements about what love is. There are many forms (types) of love. Some of the common types which you may have heard of include:

> *Eros*: erotic, passionate love
>
> *Philia*: love of friends and equals
>
> *Storge*: love of parents for children
>
> *Agape*: love of mankind

There have been many movies made about love and a multitude of books that present love stories. Much of the Bible, especially the New Testament, discusses love in terms of Christ. Many other religions emphasize the importance of love as well. Because of the great scope of the topic of love, we will concentrate mostly on some of the principles of spiritual love. We will loosely follow three of the four forms of love, Philia, Storge, and Agape, as a guideline.

Spiritual love manifests as a spiritual connection that can lead us to find meaning or purpose in our lives. Agape love and Philia love are expressed in the spiritual love that is in our soul, connecting us to all persons on the planet and to God. For those of you that don't believe in God or are uncertain about your beliefs, let's say spiritual love aligns you to the Divine Universal Energy. Spiritual love prescribes that we are all a part of God or the Divine Universal Energy and implies a Universal Oneness of all worldly and celestial manifestations. Spiritual love is love we have for our family, friends, marital partners, and significant others. This includes fellowship with neighbors and religious worshipers.

Agape love and Philia love can be seen as spiritual love that involves an alignment with our souls, our God or Divine Energy, and to humankind. We learn how to love through experience, relationships, sacrifice, giving, meditation, Bible reading, forgiveness, religious worship, and by living day-to-day in as Godlike a way as possible. After harvesting love from these sources, we then spread spiritual love to the Universe. The most enlightened form of spiritual love is expressed when we serve God and humanity without expecting anything in return. This is known as unconditional love. This is a sacrificial love that exists between man and God. Most of us are awfully familiar with this form of love because it is the same love we give to our young children. We love them unconditionally. Our love for our children is known as Storge love.

Philia love is love we have for our family, friends, marital partners, and significant others. We learn how to give and receive this love through interaction with others during our lives as infants, children, and adults. Parents that show us great love teach us how to give that same love in return. We initially give that love to our parents and will later give love outside our families.

I love you. I love you are the three most powerful words strung together in all languages around the world. When I think of my mother, I hear these three words go from her to me and from me to her. When I think of my significant other, I hear these three words go from me to her and from her to me. When I hear these three words, I hear these words go from God to me and from me to God. The words *I love you* start with a thought we create in our hearts and minds before becoming words. Love is an emotion and conscious thought before becoming a message or communication to another person, to the Universe, or to the Divine Source or God. Love is so special because it is always associated with feelings, unlike many of our other thoughts. Our average thoughts do not necessarily stir up emotion, whereas love always does.

My mother always used to say, "Michael, if you have nothing nice to say, then don't say it at all." As an adult, I have expanded this to say, "If you have nothing nice to think, then don't think it at all." It is not good enough to be loving and kind in our interactions and deeds; we must always have pure and loving thoughts as well. In this way, if we don't think hurtful thoughts, we won't say hurtful things. We can then replace hurtful thoughts and feelings with thoughts and emotions of love. We then will not scare anyone or hurt their feelings. We will not anger them, and we will not put them on the defensive. Love and other virtuous spiritual thoughts ignite loving spiritual experiences in our relationships with others.

On our holy path, our goal is to live with an increasing intensity of spiritual virtues such as love, kindness, charity, peace, and honesty. We make our existential mortal lives relatively less important and our life with Divine Energy or God most important. Love in our relationship with God, who is love, is the key to manifesting and enriching our spiritual life. When we emit total love to the Universe, the Universe returns total love to us. Our spiritual love creates Spiritual Oneness with all people of the Universe and with Divine Energy (or the Divine Energy Source) or God.

Love creates inner peace and destroys self-doubt. When we love our-selves, we are confident believers in our own thoughts and actions. We are made to feel whole. We are not fearful of what people will think of us be-cause as we give them love, they will make us feel loved in return. This makes us feel good about ourselves.

Love is selfless. We give our love without expecting anything in return. Our unconditional love for our children is known as Storge love, and our unconditional love of God is known as Agape love. When we love God unconditionally, we hope that He will help us but should never expect that He is required to oblige. Likewise, God loves us but does not anticipate our perfection. No matter what our flaws or mistakes, God still loves us. God realizes that all his children on Earth are imperfect at birth, but He trusts that we are correcting our weaknesses and spiritual mishaps throughout our human lifetime. In essence, He expects us to use our free will (which He granted us) to learn our Spiritual lessons. He created us as spiritually divine and watches us uncover our sacred authenticity as we move from the living to the Afterlife. We take on God's traits as we learn spiritual lessons in this life and the Afterlives to follow. When we eventually become the pristine spiritual love of God, we rejoin with our Creator in heaven. It is love that can quickly reunite us with God, because love is the most powerful and most important of the spiritual virtues.

When we give selfless love to those we have a relationship with, we always have their best interest in our mind and heart. We support them in any way possible and bring out the best in them. By loving ourselves, we are able to give them unconditional love.

Love for a partner is usually considered Storge love. Boorish behavior by our loved ones does not stop or change our love for them. When I give my partner selfless love, I am thinking of them first. You never expect your partner to fulfill your needs. You do your best to fulfill your partner's needs and take responsibility towards fulfilling your own needs.

Although God loves all his children equally, he is not required to take care of us. He has given us free will. The well-known adage "God helps those who help themselves" teaches us that it is not anyone else's duty, including God, to take care of us.

You must give unconditional love selflessly to your small children by fulfilling all of their needs. You will tolerate your child's abhorrent behavior more than you will tolerate anyone else's, simply because they are your child. This instinctual love for your child is the incredibly special bond between parent and child, and less so the bond of family members. Sacrifice, acceptance, and forgiveness are the hallmarks of healthy family relationships. If your wife or partner is ill from breast cancer, it is your selfless love that rises to the occasion and takes care of her needs. Putting someone's needs before your own is a challenging task, but it is part of your spiritual evolution and earns you your "wings" in the Afterlife. When both partners become selfless with each other, then we have a loving relationship where compromise between the two parties becomes easy. Being selfless is a formidable force and giving unconditional love creates a solid foundation for great relationship dynamics. Selfless love is the main characteristic of what we refer to as "true love."

Do not be judgmental of your partner who you love, or of any other person. When we judge others, we are often allowing our subconscious mind to release known flaws of our own. When we judge people, we are saying that we are better than they are. The message is that we have the right answer, and they don't. Everyone is entitled to their own beliefs and belief system. Judgment implies arrogance and a definitive lack of the spiritual virtue of humility. Being judgmental undermines love. Instead of judging others, appreciate differences in all people and simply love them for these differences. Love conquers being judgmental.

You cannot determine your partner's behavior, but you can control your own. In a loving relationship, we never try to change the partner's beliefs or personality traits. Selflessly, we should love them for who they are. If we try to change them, they will resent us, and the relationship may lead to failure. Selfless love means that "in sickness or in health," you will take care of one another.

Worry, Fear, and Love

How many of us are truly brave? When asked this question, do you think about being next to an angry bear in the woods? Do you think of a sabretooth tiger looking you squarely in the eye? Do you think of yourself as a child, afraid to enter the big new world? Does the word *fear* provoke an image of you sitting on a ledge looking down at a three-hundred-foot drop? Does your mind summon up a fear of your child becoming extremely sick or dying? Maybe your college term paper is due in three days, and you haven't started it yet. Are you worried that you will not have enough money to pay next month's bills? Are you fearful that, because of a pandemic, you may lose your employment altogether?

We all have fears, anxieties, and worries about many different things. My mother used to say, "Ninety-five percent of what we worry about never happens. The five percent we don't think of is more likely to hurt us." If my mom's adage is correct, we all waste a lot of time over fears and worries that never transpire. That is a lot of wasted energy.

For some people, worry and fear almost totally consume them. This leads to mental and physical illness. What do you do to protect yourself from worry, fear, anxiety, or maybe even panic? Panic attacks are usually the result of fear and worry that have escalated beyond one's coping mechanisms.

The first thing we must do is learn how to control our thoughts. We must mentally destroy the thought that has us worried or scared, and tell ourselves to annihilate any negative thinking immediately. We should replace the fearful thought with a more positive thought, such as the pleasantness of love. When we do this, we will immediately feel better, as thoughts of worry will slow down our heart rates and the speed of our breathing. Mental and emotional stress will diminish rapidly. As the saying goes, "Love conquers all." Sometimes it will be difficult to stop thinking about the fearful event and replace it with happier thoughts. Our brains will go right back to the worrisome thought because we are trying to release this thought without solving the underlying problem. The problem itself may be real or delusional. We think it is a severe problem, so we worry about it and become scared. Remember that my mom said that ninety-five percent of the time, what we worry about never comes to fruition. Sometimes we will solve the problem after a while, but most of the time, the problem will solve itself.

Fear and worry, along with violence and hatred, threaten our inner peace and our worldly survival. This is common when we lose our relationship with God, who is all love. The severe animosity existing between the Republican Party and the Democratic Party in The United States is the result of loss of love for each other as a people and loss of love for God. The invasion by Vladimir Putin into Ukraine can only happen because of Putin's lack of a spiritual relationship with God and his loss of love for humankind.

Let's look at some helpful ideas as to how we can get rid of our worries and fears:

Realize that this problem that has you worried may not exist, in reality.

For instance, you may be worried that because you developed a fever and a cough, you must have the coronavirus. Later you find out you had a mild case of bronchitis that went away quickly and not the coronavirus at all.

Replace fear with spiritual love for your sisters and brothers.

Think in terms of being part of a Oneness with the Universe. Friends and family who love you are there to help you get through all your problems.

Replace fear and worry with love.

Send out the message and emotion of love and direct it at the worrisome target. If you are panicked to be in a large crowd of people, tell yourself that they are your loving brothers and sisters and that you are all spiritual children of God. If you are afraid that you will not have enough money, tell yourself that the Universe is abundant, and money is coming your way.

Change your negative thinking.

Instead of throwing fear out into the Universe, bombard it with smiles, happiness, and kindness. The Law of Attraction will allow positive thoughts to result in positive experiences and your fears will diminish.

Turn to God to destroy your fear and worry.

Talk to God and say, "I am afraid of this world right now, God, and I can no longer conquer my fears myself. I am going to stop trying to fix myself and will let you help me instead. You are my supreme spiritual guide who loves me. I trust that, because you love me, you will help me find the right solution."

Use meditation to find calmness and stillness within your heart, soul, and emotions.

Meditate on seeing the worry and fear rise to the heavens, where God can help destroy this strife. Use your meditation techniques to capture any negative thoughts and feelings of worry and fear, then destroy them as soon as they enter your consciousness. Replace fearful thoughts with thoughts of love.

Let Go and Let God

Let go and let God. What does '*Let go and let God*' mean? When we have genuinely tried to do all that we can do to solve our problem or improve our circumstances, we realize that any further efforts are futile because we can no longer help ourselves. At this time, we ask God for help. We let go of trying to fix the problem ourselves and allow God to take over. Hence, *Let go and let God*. In this way, we lift up or surrender our problems to God. God is love, and we are God's children because He created us in His likeness. We must trust through faith that He will heal us and help with our difficult issues so that our inner peace can be restored. Through the Law of Attraction, as you send your message of love and faith in God through prayer or meditation, God will return love and give you answers. As a parent loves his child unconditionally, in spite of all the awful mistakes the child makes along the way, so it is with God's unconditional love for us. In God's assessment of you, you are more precious than a sapphire diamond.

When we call upon God for help, we should halt the control of our own thoughts that make up our conscious ego. Our ego mind, which is our internal dialogue, often pulls us away from pure divine understanding. While conversing with God, either through prayer or meditation, we should calm our ego mind as much as possible and allow ourselves to become silent and still. With our mind clear and our consciousness in heightened awareness, we now allow Divine Energy or God to send us the answers we need. When our ego mind is quiet, and our firm belief is that God will hear us and respond, our true essence becomes receptive to all Universal Knowledge. Answers then flow to us like a river to a waterfall. In Christianity, this spiritual empowerment created by Universal Knowledge comes to us through the Holy Spirit, who helps us find the path to God's love. In many other religions, the Holy Spirit may be referred to as simply *Spirit*. Our prayers are answered when we *Let go and let God*.

Love, Your Partner, and Death

Love is a high-quality virtue. In most religions, love is the most important virtue. Love is a relationship between families, husbands and wives, life partners, lovers, and with God. It is the most important relationship we will ever have on Earth.

Love creates inner peace and destroys war and feelings of hostility. When we are feeling and experiencing love with each other, in Oneness with the world, we augment the power of the Divine Universal Spirit. The world is at peace, and the relationship of our people with God is archetypically exemplified.

On a world scale, love is not being expressed often, and that leaves selfishness, greed, dishonesty, and power in control. Love is being expressed infrequently in the world as we do not treat our neighbors with the love and respect they deserve. Because people want to satisfy their own needs and wants, too many act selfishly, greedily, and dishonestly and try to wield their power over others. This is particularly seen among the countries and nations of the world. Instead of approaching relationships with a "win-win" philosophy, persons and nations are looking to prosper at the expense or suffering of others.

It is understood that most people, from an early age, seek out love. Yet on an individual level, there is never enough love being expressed in our personal relationships. Why is this? It is because of selfishness, greed, dishonesty, and power. Through dying, I went and looked back on my own love relationships experienced when I was alive. I learned that when I was young, I did not know how to find true, lasting love. True love is selfless. When I was alive, I was often selfish in my relationships.

As a loving partner, we must find room in our hearts for our lover's needs, ambitions, hobbies, work, family, and more. We should support our partners in their endeavors and always "have their backs." We should work to bring out the best in them as they bring out the best in us. We must address their wishes. Even when we might not agree with them, we will trust them enough to let ourselves be vulnerable when we enter into open and honest communication with them. We will recognize that they must be able to depend on our honesty. We will recognize that to maintain a healthy, loving relationship, we will both need to work diligently on it. It will sometimes not be easy work.

When love relationships begin to falter, we must ask ourselves what is going wrong. We must be honest with ourselves when we answer these questions: Are we doing our fair share of the work? Are we contributing our financial share to the household? Are we taking more than we are giving? Are we helping enough with care of the children? Are we giving?

Through your imaginary death, go back to the times of your most significant prior relationships and, while visualizing you and your lover, ask yourself these same questions and answer them honestly. Can you see where each of you could have done better to keep the love intact? As you find mistakes you made regarding things you could have done better, decide right now that you will bring this new knowledge into your current and future love relationships. Learn to choose your love partners wisely. Do not make the same mistakes again and again in the future. There is still time for true love because you are alive. I don't care if you are nineteen years old or ninety-nine years old. True love is waiting for you. You must go out and find it.

Love is the most important core value and virtue. When you are in love, you are happy, and happiness is what you deserve. When you're in love, your physical and mental health is strong and vibrant. Use your power of intention and the Law of Attraction to both find and keep a loving partner for a lifetime. Visualize your love partner with all his or her wonderful qualities. Even if you haven't met them yet, live your life as though you have already found them and live as though you are already in love. Send love out into the world daily, and love will come back to you quickly. You are not dead. You are alive and in love with yourself, the world, and your magnificent partner.

Adult Love

Here are the key points to a loving relationship between two adults:

1. Be selfless with each other.

2. Trust one another.

3. Bring out the best in each other.

4. Spend time with one another. Experience life together by doing activities with each other. Your partner should make you feel good about yourself, and you should make them feel good about themselves.

5. Always "have each other's back" when discussing each other with family and others.

6. Neither of you should totally rely on the other for your happiness. In other words, you must be happy when on your own as well. You have a life that is shared with them and a life of independence as well. This is emotionally healthy.

7. Each partner should support the other one's interests and hobbies

8. Follow the Golden Rule: "Do unto your partner as you would have them do unto you."

9. Remember that loving is giving without expecting anything in return.

10. Prioritize keeping your love strong. Work on the relationship. Relationships take a lot of work.

11. Speak to your partner with as much respect as you give your clients and co-workers.

12. Love your partner as much as yourself and your children.

13. Remember that when you feel as though your love is lost, it is possible to reignite the love between your partner and yourself.

14. Never forget the importance of loving your partner. Do not take your partner for granted. Bring love to the relationship by creating an intention to love. Use self-affirmations to solidify your love for your partner.

15. Never be judgmental of your partner.

16. Love your partner as much as you love God.

17. See if you and your partner can join in loving God together.

Obstacles to Love:

1. Making work, finances, children's issues, and other responsibilities more important than love.

2. Not spending enough "alone time" with each other.

3. Growing your interests and time in different directions from one another.

4. Smothering one another with your company. Each partner must maintain their own individuality and independence.

5. Selfishness, anger, and greed of one or both of the partners.

6. Alcohol abuse or drug addiction by one or both of the individuals. An addicted individual should seek professional assistance immediately.

7. Criticism and judgment by one or both of the individuals.

8. Saying hurtful words instead of supporting one another. Words are sometimes as hurtful as bad actions.

9. Lack of excellent communication.

10. Physical or verbal abuse. Loss of temper.

11. Depression, mental illness, or physical health issues. The mentally ill person must seek professional help immediately.

12. Lack of caring (apathy) about the relationship. Doing nothing to improve the relationship.

13. Lack of spiritual beliefs and actions, or no interest in learning spiritual lessons.

14. A lack of truthfulness with each other.

I would like to conclude this chapter with a love poem called *Love Forms*. I authored this poem especially for you.

Love Forms
I love my brothers and sisters,
There isn't any selfishness, greed, or dishonesty,
Love spreads throughout the world.

I love my children instinctively,
With all my heart and soul,
My love is unconditional.

I love my Creator,
He helps guide my spiritual path,
God speaks to me lovingly.

I love my Afterlife,
My family and friends embrace me,

I am One with God and His love.

Affirmation: "Today, I will cherish love and spread love to all the world."

Live Like You Are Dying

CHAPTER 13
Happiness

Happiness cannot be traveled to, owned, earned, worn, or consumed. Happiness is the spiritual experience of living every minute with love, grace, and gratitude.

—Denis Waitley

To enjoy good health, to bring true happiness to one's family, to bring peace to all, one must first discipline and control one's own mind. If a man can control his mind he can find a way to Enlightenment, and all wisdom and virtue will naturally come to him.

—Buddha

Happiness in the Afterlife

I feel my total being percolating with happiness in the Afterlife; I am experiencing total ecstasy. I have learned to cope with all of life's adversities, resulting in feelings of plenary bliss. I dance with jubilation when I realize I have no regrets about how I have lived. All my spiritual lessons have been met, and I rejoice! I feel the love, peace, benevolence, and grace of Jesus, and I give the same to humanity and the Divine Universe. I feel extreme pleasure knowing all my worldly possessions have been replaced with spiritual rapture. I meditate on staying true to myself, which creates euphoric emotions.

I recall the words of Yung Pueblo, as written in his book, *Inward*: "Anyone who is willing to know themselves, to face themselves with honesty and work toward loving themselves, and all beings without condition, is a hero who is adding to the collective peace of humanity" (98). I am totally true to myself and the Spiritual Universe, igniting additional pleasure and joy. With the warm cosmic light, I bake in elation when I realize I am totally free and liberated from the restrictions of living on Earth. The balance of all my Afterlife experiences fills me with feelings of happiness and victory. Greek muses dance beautifully to my right and left and sing adorable, sweet songs. They stimulate my artistic creativity, insight, and intuition. The muses conjure up euphoric dreams and fantasies of love.

I experience intense spiritual gratefulness awarded to me by Divine Oneness of the Spiritual Universe. My feelings of happiness transcend to an experience of complete elation followed by enlightenment. Full Universal Wisdom creates my ecstatic state of consciousness to the delight and ravishment of my soul. My joyous thoughts climax to supreme euphoria as all perfect solutions are made obvious. I am convinced I have arrived in either heaven or the equivalent, which is Nirvana or Jannah.

I am bathing in intense light and glowing colors. I am infused with rapture as glorious music stimulates my soul. My higher consciousness has created paradise, a sanctuary of eternal life, with illustrious gardens and beautiful visions. I relish my wisdom and the knowledge that I will live blissfully for all eternity. God and I are One, and he enlightens my total spiritual essence. I am certain I have arrived in the Kingdom of Heaven.

Joining the muses and myself, after astral projection, are my favorite angels, Clarence and Claribel. They come with those familiar smirks that always bring vital information. Upon their arrival, my clairvoyance and telepathy already tell me that I am not yet in heaven. This makes me uneasy. Then Clarence says, "You are not in heaven yet, but because of your continued goodness, you have been promoted to the next Afterlife." Then Claribel chimes in, "You must first descend to Earth and continue this book by writing a chapter on happiness." Clarence follows with, "Earthlings need to know how to find true happiness. People of the world can then spread happiness to others, and this will bring collective peace and happiness to all persons of all nations." With these words, I return to Earth to write about happiness.

Happiness

Happiness can be very elusive. Life is a series of emotional highs and lows. Just as the stock market has peaks and troughs, our happiness levels peak and wane. For a period of time, an event in our life may even make us extremely sad; I don't believe any of us can be happy all the time. Even those gurus who are able to put themselves in meditative states of bliss will eventually awaken from their peaceful higher consciousness and struggle with the pursuit of happiness.

Even though happiness can be temporary and fleeting, there are things we can do to find longer periods with greater intensity of happiness. In the previous chapters of this book, I wrote about several approaches to living that help us attain our desires, make us better human beings, and allow us to find purpose in our lives. Although I haven't spoken of happiness per se, isn't happiness really what we all desire? Let us recall some of the keywords that made up our chapter headings and recall words used frequently in this book. These include *love, meditation, health, spiritual lessons, true to oneself, Divine Energy or God, Universal Oneness, higher consciousness, giving, Spiritual Balance, The Law of Attraction, positive thinking, gratefulness, peace,* and *calmness.* Aren't these subjects and practices a means to find happiness? Let us examine the ways we can successfully pursue and find happiness by focusing on some key points of these previously established ideas.

Positive Thinking

Abraham Lincoln said, "Man is about as happy as he makes up his mind to be." This statement implies that we control our own happiness. Too often, we think that unfortunate events and unfeeling people are the causes of our unhappiness. Paradoxically, it is our avoidable reactions that result in our unhappiness. Unhappiness is the result of choosing negative thinking over positive thinking. Norman Vincent Peale was a Protestant minister and famous inspirational author who was known as one of the greatest positive thinkers of modern times. He authored the book, *The Power of Positive Thinking*. In this book, his formula for happiness encompassed optimism with Christian faith. The book talks about a man who carried a card that read, "The way to happiness: Keep your heart free from hate, your mind from worry. Live simply, expect little, give much. Fill your life with love. Scatter sunshine. Forget self, think of others. Do as you would be done by. Try this for a week and you will be surprised" (Peale 63).

Doctor Peale further commented on happiness, "In other words, cultivate the merry heart; that is, develop the happiness habit, and life will become a continual feast, which is to say you can enjoy life every day. Out of the happiness habit comes a happy life" (60). Most psychologists and sociologists now accept the belief that positive thinking leads to reduced stress levels, better physical health, reduction of self-doubt, greater success, and increased happiness.

The Law of Attraction

Napoleon Hill, a great author of the laws of success, wrote in the book, *Think and Grow Rich,* "Whatever the mind of man can conceive and believe it can achieve" (32). When we set goals for ourselves that we are passionate about, and positive feelings of excitement and joy are stimulated, we reach overall happiness. Our thoughts and actions are steps on our spiritual journey that bring emotional fulfillment, making us happier than reaching the actual destination, known as our goal. With conviction and commitment, which are deep intentional drives to reach our desired goal, we evoke pleasurable emotions and consequently achieve our desired aspirations. Our positive commitments define who we become. Happiness is reached by both the process and discipline required during the necessary work, and again when the goal is achieved. The means is often more enjoyable than the end event.

Simply setting goals is not usually enough for success and happiness. We must visualize being in possession of our achievement, which in turn triggers powerful emotions of excitement, pride, joy, and happiness, making the desired goal extremely likely. With deep conviction in our goal that has meaning to us, along with arousal of positive emotions and visualization, we experience happiness.

Tal Ben-Shahar, Ph.D., makes the additional point that meaningful goals require both future and present benefit. In his book, *Happier*, he summarizes, "We need the experience of meaning and the experience of positive emotions; we need present and future benefits" (43). I agree with this latter point regarding present and future benefits. The goal becomes most emotionally fulfilling and contributes to greater happiness when it is both enjoyed by the work in the present and further enjoyed by a meaningful destination in the future.

Regrets

When elderly people in the later stages of their life were asked about their happiness level, those who had few or no regrets about the life they'd lived were happier than those who had regrets. In his book, *The Five Secrets You Must Discover Before You Die.*, John B. Izzo writes, "Many of us live our entire lives hiding under the desk, believing that failure and rejection are the worst that can happen to us. Yet these two hundred interviews have brought me to a different conclusion, that the thing we ought to fear most is the regret of having not tried" (54). We must not allow worry or fear of failure to deter us from aspiring to achieve our most authentic aspirations and dreams. We must continuously strive for the meaning in our life by aspiring to achieve our calling.

Happiness during life and near the end of life is greatly determined by whether or not we have regrets. Although these can take the form of aspirations and goals we were fearful of trying to achieve, they can also involve regrets of apologies never given or forgiveness never granted. If you need to "come clean" with some folks, do it now. If you have a "bucket list" of dreams you want to accomplish before the end of your life, do them now. Do you have any regrets at this moment? What must you do in your life going forward so you will have few or no regrets later on in life? Answer these questions and act as soon as possible. You will be playing an active role in creating your own happiness.

I had a dream that I was treating a fifty-five-year-old man in the hospital who was in respiratory failure. He had smoked cigarettes for forty years and developed chronic obstructive pulmonary disease (COPD) and now also suffered from pulmonary hypertension. He was receiving oxygen and his breathing was horrifically strained. He said to me, "I regret having smoked all those years. I did this to myself." At that moment, I felt a sadness that was more intense than any sadness I had ever experienced before. When I awoke and remembered my dream, I decided to pray for all those lost souls who had intense regrets. Please, cross over to your Afterlife without regrets.

I had another dream two days later. This time it was about a woman who had not spoken to her daughter in 20 years. She had not seen her grandchildren since they were born. In the dream, she cried and said, "I regret I couldn't find a way to reconcile with my daughter. I have lost so much precious time." When I awoke, that was all I could remember. I then decided to pray for all the people of the world who have regrets regarding relationships with family members. I prayed rigorously for these folks every night for six weeks. Please, do not cross over to your Afterlife with regrets.

Bucket List

A bucket list is a list of all those things you want to experience or achieve in your lifetime before crossing over to your Afterlife. It may include traveling to Europe, giving to a foundation, getting married, or reading the Bible. Create your own bucket list now, and start fulfilling all your own wishes and achievements. Achieving these goals will lead to great happiness because you will not die with the regret of not having made these things a reality.

While performing the actions on your bucket list, feel proud of all you are experiencing and achieving.

Good Health

Start to exercise and eat well if you are not already. If you already are, think of ways you can increase your exercise performance and eat even healthier foods. Go for regular checkups with your internist and call the doctor if you are concerned with a physical or mental problem you are currently experiencing. Make sure you have health insurance and have your teeth taken care of. Much physical suffering and pain occur when folks neglect their own health. You must not live your life in pain. If you have chronic pain, know that there is medical help available. Do not believe that pain is just something with which you must live.

Many health issues can be prevented. You are your own best health advocate. Your physical body is your temple that houses the Spirit, and all of your physical actions, mental thoughts, and spiritual endeavors are dependent on its proper function. Without good health, you have nothing—because you cannot experience all that life has to offer. Without good health, all the money and material possessions in the world are useless to you. Your happiness depends on your ongoing good health.

Relationship with Divine Energy or God

When my relationship with God is strong, I never feel alone. He is with me to tackle every one of life's adversities or setbacks that is thrown my way. He empowers me to have courage, insight, and intuition when life becomes challenging and problems begin to mount. When I speak with God in prayer, he allows answers to questions to surface in my higher consciousness. I have faith in God that things will turn out okay. I am confident that God's Divine Energy will make Universal Knowledge and Universal Wisdom accessible to me so that solutions are readily available. If things become so bad that I feel lost, dejected, and full of despair, I stop trying to make things better by myself and turn it over to God for the remedy. I "let go and let God." Through faith, I know God will never let me down. Dark skies will diminish, and blue skies with his brilliant light will again bring forth my inevitable happiness. To keep me strong and optimistic during grim times, I affirm Psalm 23:4 of the Bible, "Even when I walk through the darkest valley, I will not be afraid, for you are close behind me. Your rod and your staff protect and comfort me."

There was a thirty-five-year-old man who had a five-year-old son. The man had always been very spiritual and had a firm belief in God. About six months earlier, the man's five-year-old son developed a rapid, insidious illness and died. The man had been very depressed since his child's death six months ago. He would ask God, "Why would you let this happen to my son? You have allowed my life to be destroyed." The man would often cry himself to sleep. He was driving to the store one sunny day when the sky was very blue. As he was slowing down for an upcoming red light, the song "Amazing Grace" began to play on the radio. This was always his favorite spiritual song. As the music played, he began to feel that God was nearby. When he arrived at the red light and stopped the car, a man about his age, extremely tall (about 6'6") with extremely long arms, was crossing the street with his son. His son looked about five years old and was so much like his own son, they could have passed for twins. At the precise moment that they reached the center of his car's hood, the tall man lifted his son high above his head with his long, extended arms and smiled. It appeared the man was lifting the boy to the heavens. Just then, the white, puffy clouds on the bright, blue sky separated, and a brilliant beam of light appeared, as though coming straight from the heavens. The light created a great illumination of the man and his child. "Amazing Grace" played louder in the background. The man in the car knew with certainty that this was a Spiritual Synchronicity created by God to tell him that his son was in a better place. The man's faith was restored as he knew God was sending the message that, in time, he would live again with his son in the Afterlife. He now felt that God was not responsible for his son's death. Soon afterwards, the man was lifted out of his depression. In time, his spiritual growth became stronger than ever, and he went on to enjoy a happy life.

Giving

I used to think that giving meant giving away your money. While being raised in the Catholic faith and later going to Protestant churches, I always heard Christians say to tithe ten percent of the money you have. I was never enthusiastic about this idea and never gave this much. It is important to understand that there are several ways to be giving, and all of these can be very meaningful.

Benevolence is a form of giving. When we are kind and supportive of those in need, we are giving emotional support to others. If we work as a volunteer in a food pantry for several hours, this form of kindness to others is spiritual giving. When we give our love, our knowledge, and our possessions, we give others joy and will find happiness for ourselves.

Giving includes the giving of one's time. If I work in a hospital, keeping dying patients company, I am giving of my time. Philanthropy can mean giving monetarily, but it can also mean giving of one's time.

Giving includes helping others in many ways. When we give advice, we are also giving. If I give of my talents that benefit others, I am using my knowledge and ability to be giving. When I worked in dermatology, we would sometimes give free skin examinations for half a day. This volunteer function would help find skin issues people didn't know they had and would also encourage people to have yearly skin checks performed by a dermatologist. In this way, skin cancers could be found that otherwise would have gone undetected. We were giving of our medical expertise to the public free of charge.

There is always joy in giving. When we give of ourselves to people and the Universe, rewards taking any number of forms will be returned to us. You may receive love, knowledge, monetary gain, happiness, or something else, as the Universe reciprocates. H. Jackson Brown, in *Complete Life's Little Instruction Book*, said it best: "Remember that the happiest people are not those getting more, but those giving more" ("H. Jackson Brown Quotes" qtd. in Brown). Giving more than we receive is one of life's spiritual lessons. It can be learned in the Afterlife, but it is best to learn it in this lifetime.

Coping

Your relationship with Divine Energy or God is the number one personal belief that will bring you happiness all your life. Your coping mechanism ability (sometimes referred to as resilience) is the most important trait or ability that will determine your intensity of happiness and frequency of happiness. The ability to react positively and constructively to life's occasionally terrible circumstances is paramount to keeping sadness and despair short-lived and returning to happiness as quickly as possible. When we discover and utilize our skill of bouncing back from life's inevitable setbacks, happiness can practically approach a constant in our emotional state.

Take the example of a woman who has cheated on her long-time boyfriend. Depending on the boyfriend's ability to cope with the situation, he may react by becoming extremely angry and may stalk her. He may become violent with the woman or her lover. If the boyfriend were a different person who had good coping skills, he might become angry or sad at first but would control his emotions and make a decisive, positive plan of action. He would either reestablish his relationship with the woman (with the lover out of the picture) or break up with her and move on. With good coping skills, he would not allow this event to lead him into depression and despair; instead, he creates a better situation, and his happiness is restored.

Coping with life's problems and learning how to react in constructive and effective ways to adverse experiences can be immensely difficult for certain individuals. The study of coping mechanism development is extremely complex and goes beyond the scope of this book. I will, however, give some quick general advice on coping with adversity.

Don't become fixated on the current problem. Most big issues in your life take a while to resolve. Many of them will go away on their own, so don't spend all your time worrying or being unhappy. If you can do something to remedy the situation, create a good plan and perform it quickly. The faster you solve the problem, the quicker you can return to happiness. If possible, "Make lemons out of lemonade." We can often find solutions to problems if we think creatively. Keep your attitude and reactions towards adversity as positive as possible. By using your higher consciousness and ability to meditate, wipe out all of your negative thinking. Remember that coping with problems involves insight, creativity, intellect, and intuition. If you are unable to cope with a horrific situation, turn it over to Divine Energy or God to solve. Recall that no problem exists beyond death. A worry-free Afterlife is inevitable.

By utilizing the concepts discussed in this book, such as meditation, spiritual growth, positive thinking, creativity, intuition, and positive self-esteem, you will become better at coping with adversity almost automatically. Consequentially, your emotional state will most often be one of happiness.

Freedom

Those who are enslaved—either by themselves or by others—will rarely find happiness. Whether you are physically or emotionally enslaved, happiness will always be elusive. Throw off the mental shackles that confine creative thinking. Do not let prejudice, anger, judgment, dislike, despair, fear, or worry impede your success or happiness.

There is a direct correlation between freedom and happiness. In the online article, "The Connection Between Freedom and Happiness," the nationwide General Social Survey (undertaken by the National Opinion Research Center) revealed that people who said they felt completely or very free were twice as likely to say they were incredibly happy about their lives than those who felt only a moderate degree of freedom or less (Vaz). People want the freedom to make their own decisions and pursue their own goals. This probably does not surprise many of us Americans, as we think of our freedoms and our rights fairly often. In our American culture, we have become very "constitutionally aware."

What we don't think about often is our freedom and happiness after death. Death is the most freeing of all of life's events, when we are released from the restriction of our physical bodies. In death, we are set free from all worldly problems. We are released from financial debt, free of pain and suffering, and liberated from all rules, laws, and restrictions. The Afterlife has no Democratic and Republican parties. Our governing bodies are replaced with Divine Energy or God. There is also no restriction as to time or place and no travel restrictions. Death is the total liberation of the soul. Our temporary Earthly possessions are replaced with a meaningful spiritual life filled with love, kindness, and integrity. The fear of death is replaced with the knowledge of eternal life, resulting in bliss.

Internal Peace and Calmness

Peace of mind is essential to experience happiness. When the mind and emotions are peaceful, so is the body. With the body, the mind, and the emotions calm and peaceful, happiness will either be present or will be about to take hold.

The Bible is full of references to calmness and peace because we are told that God can grant these important states of mind. They are key to our overall joy and happiness. Jesus's statement about peace reads, "I am leaving you a gift—peace of mind and heart. And the peace I give you is a gift the world cannot give. So don't be troubled or afraid " (John 14.27).

Death on Earth is the ultimate peace and calmness, as we are completely free of all of life's turmoil. The Afterlife will give us peace and tranquility that far exceed worldly peace.

Be True to Yourself

Become aware of your heart's desire. What is your calling in life? What do you want your present and future to look like? What do you need to do to bring meaning to your life? Get in touch with your authentic self. Your authentic self comes from your heart and your soul. Your authentic self is full of joy. When you were a child, and more recently, what brought you the most happiness? If you have always loved math, science, and the workings of the human body, then go into medicine or scientific research. If you have always loved dancing, consider opening a dance school. Always reaffirm to yourself those elements in life that you find most important. Write down your purpose in life and affirm it daily. Meditate and pray on your purpose in life. Devise a plan and a path to accomplish your goals. Revise your plan as needed with time. Think about how your life's work can become more meaningful by contributing to loved ones and to society.

Are you doing things you shouldn't be doing, although you know they are wrong? Do you know smoking is wrong, but you do it anyway? Do you know lying in business or lying on your taxes is wrong, but you do it because you will get away with it? Do you drive and text but know you shouldn't because it increases the odds of a car accident? Do you know drinking and driving is wrong, but you have convinced yourself nothing will happen because you know what you are doing? Say no to yourself and others when you know it is wrong!

Are you doing what you want, or are you influenced by what others advise? Make sure you are making up your own mind. People who know themselves are confident about what they need and should do. You should obtain information from other people and sources before a decision is made, but the final decision should be yours.

Lead a righteous life with honesty, fairness, kindness, and love, and you will find you are always true to yourself. This will bring you long-term happiness. A reverent person is who you truly are. When you don't live this way, you are not being true to yourself. If you don't learn life's spiritual lessons, your actions will have consequences. The man who cheats on his wife and drinks too much liquor will eventually pay for the poor decisions he makes. He may find himself divorced and/or hospitalized. Learn the spiritual lessons (Chapter 2) and live by them. Learning them now will mean you will need to learn less, or nothing, in your Afterlife.

These endeavors will help you to never lose sight of who you are. These actions will lead to successful, happy living.

Gratitude

Finding happiness by becoming a grateful person goes way beyond saying "thank you." We become truly and honestly grateful when we count our blessings instead of focusing on what we don't have.

Let's take our place of employment as our first example of gratefulness and how it relates to our happiness. We can approach our jobs by concentrating on the things we like about our jobs or on the things we hate about our jobs. We can plan on developing our jobs into a more enjoyable workplace for ourselves, or we can give up and say to ourselves, "I am stuck in a job I don't like and there is nothing that will change this." In one of my later jobs, working as a physician assistant as a state employee, I found myself beginning to focus on the lack of pay increases and the administration not appreciating what I was contributing to the department. Those negative thoughts at work were beginning to make me unhappy. I decided to get out of this rut by developing better relationships with my patients and finding boundless joy in my interactions with them. Very quickly, I became happy while working because I was so grateful to have the opportunity to take care of my patients.

Let's look at gratefulness in primary relationships. When a relationship with our spouse or significant other becomes strained (and this is inevitable), there is a quick and effective solution. Focus on your partner's positive traits and contributions to the relationship instead of the things they do that aggravate you. Do not concentrate on traits you don't like about them.

Begin to appreciate and become grateful for having them in your life. By focusing on all your partner's positive qualities and attributes instead of all of your negative attitudes towards them, your gratefulness will create your happiness.

Become grateful for being alive and for your inevitable death into new life. Every day, thank God for the beautiful day ahead of you. The Holy Bible says, "This is the day the Lord has made. We will rejoice and be glad in it " (Ps 118.24). By entering each day with a positive attitude and gratefulness to Divine Energy or God, you will create joy and happiness in your daily experiences. Look at the wonderful day and enjoy all of nature that surrounds you. Then, focus on all the people in your life—the family and friends for whom you are grateful. Be grateful for all the possessions that you have been blessed with. Try your best not to focus on the things you don't have. In this way, the things you want and need will be given to you by the abundance of Universal Energy.

Although your future death may seem sad, try to embrace it now. Birth and death are more a part of worldly spiritual life than anything else. Keep telling yourself that death is not an end, but the beginning of a greater life. If you lose a loved one, be grateful to the Universe or God for the time you've had with them on Earth. Use your higher consciousness to accept through faith the knowledge that you will join them again in one of your Afterlives. Most of all, agree that by reading this book, you now understand that the birth-death continuum is joyous. Having learned this Universal Divine knowledge, you can now be grateful, emotionally fulfilled, and have a happier life.

Balance and Living in the Moment

You have already read a chapter on balance and Spiritual Balance earlier in this book. Learning to be aware of the importance of balance and then practicing it are skills that will add to your happiness. Recall that when we become extreme about anything, we set ourselves up for an emotional fall.

When we focus our lives intensely on one or two endeavors, to the exclusion of everything else, sadness finds its way into our hearts. The archetypical example of lack of balance in life is when someone spends almost all their time working and thinking about working. Their relationships with their spouse and children will then suffer. The spouse who works sixteen hours a day, six days a week, completely misses his children's childhood.

Another key to keeping balance in your life to maintain satisfaction and happiness is the concept of time. When we balance our priorities, time takes its normal course. If our priorities are unbalanced, we run out of time quickly. This happens because we never have enough time to get things done. A person who spends an inordinate amount of time traveling because his employment requires it loses time to fulfill his personal obligations.

When our life's practical functions and our daily thoughts are not in equilibrium with all the many responsibilities and demands of life, we begin to live in the past and future instead of in the moment. When we disparage balance in our lives, we never "stop to smell the roses." We lose focus on everything else life offers us at that given moment. We become driven by future deadlines and monetary goals. It becomes difficult to enjoy the present because our thoughts are only focused on our future activity. When we live in the present, we do not worry if we did things correctly in the past, nor do we worry about what will take place in the future. When we are constantly working toward future goals, we forget to enjoy life right now.

By living in the moment, you can get things done. As the well-known adage reminds us, "do not put off for tomorrow what can be done today, because tomorrow may never come." The future is uncertain, and the past cannot be changed, but you can make a difference right now in the present. Become not only a thinker but become a doer. Everything gets accomplished by activity. All activities are performed in the present and not the future. This is because, by the time future activities are performed, they are part of the present. By keeping a balance between past, present, and future activities, you will maintain happiness. Always respect and become aware of the necessity of simple tenses (past, present, and future), but make your present moment the highest priority and the most valuable. Balance does not always mean equal proportions. Sometimes the correct balance is to have more of one than the other. For example, we have a healthy living balance when we have sixteen waking hours and eight sleeping hours.

Balance your ego life with your spiritual life. Your life of work, child-rearing, and personal pleasure activities are important, but do not neglect your spiritual growth. Decide for yourself how much you need of each.

Think about your practical activities and your entire secular life, but spend some time thinking about your inevitable death. Do not avoid or be fearful of leaving your worldly possessions behind. Do not be fearful of the Crossover to your Afterlife. Utilize some of your time to become as prepared as possible for this consequential and purposeful event. Please do not think of your death as a non-event or something that will happen far in the future. Our time spent in this world is uncertain. By balancing thoughts of life and death in meaningful ways, we can have the satisfaction that we are well prepared for our demise. We should be spiritually prepared for the lessons we're about to learn in the next life. This is part of the Spiritual Balance of life.

Meditation

You will find happiness by meditating. It is recommended that you meditate daily, but you will find the right amount for you. Since a previous chapter was devoted to meditation, we will not go into great detail.

Here are some of the potential benefits of meditation:

1. **A Reduction in Stress** — Meditation brings a reduction in stress and an increase in intensity and frequency of feelings of happiness. Some folks may even experience fleeting moments of rapture or bliss during meditations. You will experience calm and peace.

2. **Reaching a Higher Consciousness** — There is also a previous chapter devoted to this subject, so we will avoid going into detail. Recall that higher consciousness allows for greater awareness, insight, and intuition and promotes happiness and well-being.

3. **Better Health** — Improvements in physical and mental health can result from meditation. Fear, worry, and anxiety will decrease during and after meditation. In the *Journal of Clinical Psychology*, Elizabeth Hoge's research abstract, "Randomized Controlled Trial of Mindfulness Meditation for General Anxiety Disorder: Effects on Anxiety and Stress Reactivity," studied the effects of mindful meditation on Stress Reduction and Generalized Anxiety Disorder. The conclusion was the following: "The results suggest that Mindful-Based Stress Reduction (MBSR) may have a beneficial effect on anxiety symptoms in Generalized Anxiety Disorder (GAD) and may also improve stress reactivity and coping as measured in a laboratory stress challenge" (786-792). Additionally, people who meditate will usually sleep better. This contributes to good health. Meditation has also been shown to decrease blood pressure.

4. **Spiritual Growth** — For many, meditation will lead to spiritual growth. The reasons for this are probably diverse. Some people decide to meditate on spiritual virtues and send out love to people and to the Universe. Several studies have demonstrated that people increase their kindness after meditating. The more time people spend meditating, the more loving and benevolent they become. Many people find the meditation experience elicits feelings of kindness, love, compassion, rapture, and more. While meditating, you may realize that your physical body is not your true self, but your Spirit is. Many people find that meditation is a metaphysical or spiritual experience because it brings them closer to Divine Energy or God.

5. **Improved Feelings about Death** — By meditating on your death and rebirth, you may gain an innovative approach to living. Meditation will help you lose your fear of death.

All of these benefits of meditation will help to increase your overall happiness.

Affirmation: "I am truly happy when I fully enjoy each breathing moment of my life."

CHAPTER 14
Jesus Christ and Multiple Religions

Jesus replied, 'You must love the Lord your God with all your heart, all your soul, and all your mind.' This is the first and greatest commandment. A second is equally important: 'Love your neighbor as yourself.' The entire law and all the demands of the prophets are based on these two commandments.

—Matthew 22.37–40

Jesus and God in the Afterlife

I am still not in heaven, but I am in my third Afterlife. Of late, most of my actions and deeds are of the highest spiritual quality. I feel I am remarkably close to reaching the Kingdom of Heaven. I feel my ego mind is at rest, and I continuously use my higher consciousness with pure spiritual thought.

I meet with Jesus today, and I am surprised by how calm and peaceful I feel when I am with him. As usual, he mostly speaks to me in parables, as this is his modus operandi. He often starts his sentences with, "I will tell you the truth," which is unnecessary as I would never doubt his words. He usually seems profoundly serious. This time is no different. He turns toward me and says, "You must astral project to the Garden of Eden to learn some important spiritual information." Although I never feel like leaving Jesus, I do as he says. I depart and soon become eager to reach the Garden.

Arriving in the Garden of Eden, I see the "forbidden fruit" growing from the "tree of the knowledge of good and evil" (Gen. 2.17). The villainous serpent is nearby. The Garden itself has the beauty of paradise. A semicircular, colorful rainbow is in the sky, and to my left, there is a magnificent, serene waterfall gently splashing down onto the floor of the Garden. Eden is full of all kinds of colorful flowers, including red roses, tall yellow and pink tulips, a multitude of yellow marigolds, lavender hydrangeas, and assorted colors of begonias. I spot Adam and go to him to introduce myself. He is very handsome and loquacious. Both of us talk and then look for Eve but are unable to find her. I feel disappointed not to see her.

An entity of Divine Energy appears and begins to communicate his message in the most confident frequency. He tells me he is God the Father. His voice radiates through all of Eden, and Adam looks frightened. God exclaims, "To enter the Kingdom of Heaven, you must follow the teachings of myself and Jesus, the Son of Man. A man's deeds must be virtuous, and he must live by my Commandments. No evil person will enter my Kingdom." I am extremely grateful for this spiritual lesson and ask God the Father, "Can someone enter the kingdom without taking Jesus as their Savior?" God replies, "All will declare Jesus Christ and I as their God before entering the Kingdom of Heaven." My meek, shivering voice says, "Thank you, Lord."

Feeling that Jesus was more popular and prominent in the Christian faith, and God the Father was not given equal importance, I descended to Earth to write one of my last chapters, "Christ and Multiple Religions."

Jesus Christ

Let me make it clear that I am not dead. Although I speak of my death in this book, I am very much alive. I am a living Christian. Although I was born into Catholicism, I became a Christian and accepted Jesus Christ as my Savior during my early adult years, because Christianity became my spiritual path, as I will explain soon.

I was born into Roman Catholicism and my parents had me baptized as an infant by a priest in the church. Sunday mass was a ritual for most of my childhood years. When I was in my early twenties, I began to read personal growth (self-help) books. Many of these books had spiritual and religious undertones. When I came across Dr. Norman Vincent Peale's book, *The Power of Positive Thinking*, I found a synergy between personal optimism and Jesus Christ as my path to spiritual happiness and success. During that time, I probably read about thirty books by Dr. Peale. When I found out he was still giving sermons at Marble Collegiate Church in New York City, I began to attend his services every Sunday morning. Fortunately for me, I happened to live in Manhattan at the time as I was attending a physician assistant school at New York Hospital on 59th Street. I discovered that I enjoyed the Dutch Reformed Congregation (a Protestant Church) far more than the Roman Catholic Church. In the Dutch Reformed Church, there was far less reference to "fire and brimstone." I was later baptized by a minister of the Dutch Reformed Church, into Christ's world, as a young adult. I reaffirmed my belief that Jesus Christ is my Savior. I agreed to live a righteous life of Christianity and serve Jesus. I read the New Testament of the Bible several times and attended multiple Bible study classes. My spiritual journey became a Christian path.

Christians are extremely Bible-oriented. For Christians, the Bible is the Word of God. At a minimum, it is the *inspired* Word of God. Christians also believe that salvation can only be attained through Jesus Christ, the Son of God (also known as the Son of Man). Salvation is the deliverance from sin and its consequences; when taking Jesus as your Savior, your sins are forgiven. In eternal life (heaven), the Christian has everlasting peace, love, and happiness.

Many evangelical Christians will not agree that I am living as a Christian. I say this because, although I believe Jesus has saved me, I believe in multiple Afterlives. Christians would say that since I believe Christ has saved me, I should believe I will go straight to heaven. Multiple Afterlives is not a Christian belief.

Even though I have been baptized in Jesus's name twice in my life, I may or may not go straight to heaven. If I demonstrate poor spiritual behavior through my actions, Jesus and God will not permit my immediate entrance into heaven. To bypass multiple Afterlives and go to heaven as soon as I leave Earth, my spiritual intentions must be heartfelt, and all my spiritual lessons must be displayed in my actions.

I believe my spiritual lessons must be learned and lived before I will be ready to enter the Kingdom of Heaven. In Matthew, Chapter 5, Jesus says:

> *So, if you ignore the least Commandment and teach others to do the same, you will be called the least in the Kingdom of Heaven. But anyone who obeys God's laws and teaches them will be called great in the Kingdom of Heaven. But I warn you—unless your righteousness is better than the righteousness of the teachers of religious law and the Pharisees, you will never enter the Kingdom of Heaven! (Matt. 5.19-20)*

In these verses, Christ makes it clear that it is through righteousness that we enter the Kingdom of Heaven.

Christ is the immediate doorway to eternal life. The problem is that not all of us are ready to accept Jesus Christ, the Son of Man, as our Savior. Some of us may find Jesus now, but others will come to know him later in this lifetime, while still others will not find him until crossing over to the Afterlife. There may even be some who take more than one Afterlife to understand that by believing that Jesus Christ is the Son of God (Son of Man), they will reach the Kingdom of Heaven.

You may ask, "Why don't you believe that people must find Jesus in this lifetime to be saved or become damned for all eternity?" Firstly, if someone leads a wonderful and reverent life as a loving person, and believes in God, don't they deserve a better outcome than damnation when they die? What kind of God, who by definition is all-good, would disallow such a fine person from eternal happiness when they have loved God all their life? A follower with a strong relationship with God, who serves God for his lifetime but is never comfortable receiving the "body and blood of Christ," should not receive the punishment of eternal damnation.

Let's look at why Christians should be tolerant of those who have not found Jesus Christ as their Savior yet. Historically, it has been shown that several unknown authors wrote the New Testament and possibly the Gospels of Matthew, Mark, Luke, and John. Therefore, we cannot be sure that Jesus' disciples and apostles successfully conveyed the words and messages intended. All of their accounts of Jesus in the New Testament are different. Matthew's quotes of Jesus mostly refer to the need for people to trust and believe in God, and they speak little about Jesus being the only way to eternal life. John, on the other hand, has a conviction that followers will only find eternal life through their belief in Jesus. Note that Jesus never directly authored anything the Bible gives him credit for. All of Jesus's words in the New Testament come from authors/scribes other than himself.

Much of what the authors quote Jesus as saying is focused on living a life that follows the Ten Commandments and God's messages. Jesus wants us to refrain from evil and murder. Many of Christ's quotes tell us to believe in God the Father with all our heart. He says many times that God the Father and himself are the same. He encourages us to pray to and believe in God to have eternal life. In Matthew, Jesus said, "Not everyone who calls out to me, "Lord, Lord!" will enter the Kingdom of Heaven. Only those who actually do the will of my Father in heaven will enter. On judgment day many will say to me, "Lord Lord!" we prophesied in your name, and cast out demons in your name and performed many miracles in your name." But I will reply, "I never knew you. Get away from me, you who break God's laws" (Matt. 7.21-23). This statement confirms Jesus's conviction that we go to heaven not only through him, but also through God the father. Jesus also is clear that following him and God the Father is not enough. We must also not break God's laws.

Let me make it clear that I do not believe in reincarnation into another human life or animal life. I believe that when you are reborn into your next Afterlife, you are born into a non-physical body, which becomes a spiritual being with a higher level of consciousness. We spiritually evolve to new planes of existence by learning and practicing our spiritual lessons. After dying, the spiritual virtues, especially love, replace feelings of greed, anger, jealousy, and resentment. When our souls are purified by our virtuous behavior, we are then ready to enter the Kingdom of Heaven.

The main purpose of my book is not to encourage people to accept Christ as their Savior, although it would be wonderful if this happened. People will go to Christ in their own time. I authored this book to encourage people to live spiritually virtuous lives so that they can find good health and happiness. When people live righteous lives, a collective peace and cooperation of humanity glorifies God's wishes. This, of course, is what Spiritual Oneness is all about. My hope is that this book brings more people to God, for this is an important spiritual lesson necessary to reach heaven. The spiritual lesson here is to make God the most important purpose of your life.

I believe in Jesus Christ as my Savior because I have faith in him. It is not strictly based on the Word of God in the Bible. Above all else, religion is a faith because there isn't any empirical evidence of God. There is no scientific proof that Jesus is the Son of Man and the only way to find salvation. I believe in Jesus because I speak to him, and he listens. He is my Savior because he has answered my prayers all my life. I have used my intuition, the answered prayers, meditations, and faith to conclude that Jesus died for me so that I may have eternal life. For this, I love him with all my heart. I will not, however, judge anyone who does not accept him as their Savior because Jesus has always taught me not to judge others. Although we can evangelize to others about Jesus, we should always demonstrate humility because this is what Jesus also teaches us. We must never tell non-believers they will be left for dead or punished forever unless they acknowledge that only Jesus can save their souls. Each person will learn that Jesus Christ is Lord when their spirit is ripe for it. No one with love in their heart, who has lived a Godlike life, will be denied eternity.

The idea that there can be multiple Afterlives without our physical forms came to me over time. It came to me through intuition, meditation, prayer, and common sense. Historically, the Roman Catholic's concept of purgatory comes close to the concept of an Afterlife that is neither heaven nor hell. Some people take more than one physical world experience to get spiritual growth right. For other people, it will take more than one non-physical Afterlife experience to learn Jesus Christ is their Messiah. The Bible says, "Don't be surprised! Indeed, the time is coming when all the dead in their graves will hear the voice of God's Son, and they will rise again. Those who have done good will rise to experience eternal life, and those who have continued in evil will rise to experience judgment" (John 5.28-29). Maybe, this scripture is telling us that when Jesus comes again to judge the living and the dead, people who are in their Afterlives will be included. All non-believers who have passed on will have another chance to accept Jesus as their Savior.

Our world consists of so much devotion to material possessions, competition, greed, and violence. Finding a reverent, spiritual path has become difficult for many. We must have patience with those who struggle with religious beliefs and spiritual endeavors. God the Father came to me in my prayers and told me to bring people to God. He said to remind people that goodness and living the spiritual virtues are paramount to good health, peace, and finding everlasting life. It is clear that God wants his son Jesus to save mankind, but God never told me to write a book only about Jesus—not yet, anyway. If this authorship helps even a few people reconnect with God and live a pure, spiritual life filled with joy, I will be happy I undertook it.

Multiple Religions

Hinduism

Let's say I am born into a different life and take a vastly different spiritual path. Imagine I am born and raised in the Hindu religion. What is my Afterlife like? In Hinduism, there is a belief in a rebirth cycle known as reincarnation. Karma is defined as people's actions or deeds while living, which have spiritual consequences in their Afterlife. The individual's degree of good deeds will determine the type of entity he will be born into in the next life. All good behaviors and bad behaviors in this life result in either rewards or punishment (fitting to the bad behavior) in the next Afterlife.

All Hindus believe they have multiple Afterlives. The Hindu knows his soul will find a new physical form in each new Afterlife. The physical form may be that of an animal (since they believe animals have souls) or that of a man. Some Hindus also believe in the caste system, which is a hierarchy of social stratification. Hindus at the top of the hierarchy have many more privileges and receive more respect than those at the lower levels.

As a Hindu, I believe in rejoining with God. To rejoin with God, I attain a blissful state without pain or suffering. Each time I become a new physical entity through reincarnation, my soul gets closer to perfection, as almost all my deeds are righteous, and my spiritual lessons have been learned. After many excellent spiritual reincarnations, my godlike spirit transpires, and I am no longer in need of physical reincarnations. I have now reached "Moksha," a blissful plane of consciousness. This is the Hindu version of heaven. My soul, as a Hindu, is free from the birth-death continuum. All karmas have been resolved, and I am One with God. Hinduism believes that every person on Earth can reach Moksha. Hindus are very open-minded and respect and appreciate all religious beliefs. They do not believe in eternal damnation.

Unlike Christianity, Hinduism does not claim there is one single book that contains the word of God. Some of their cherished scriptures include the Bhagavad-Gita and the four Vedas. Although Hindus may worship many gods, there is a core triad of three gods worshiped in Hinduism: Brahma, Vishnu, and Shiva. Krishna is a beloved incarnation of Vishnu and, although he inhabited the Earth in human form around 315 B.C., he is believed to be a God (Rahul).

Buddhism and its Similarities to Hinduism

Let's say, this time I am born in China, and I am raised as a Buddhist. China has 18% of all the world's Buddhists. I still believe in karma and reincarnation. I know that I will have many Afterlives. Both Buddhists and Hindus believe in "Samsara," an almost endless cycle of birth-death-rebirth. I will break the cycle of Samsara by learning my spiritual lessons, also known as enlightenment. Good behavior or moral order is called "Dharma" in both religions. For Buddhists, reaching enlightenment is known as Nirvana and for the Hindus it is known as Moksha, as previously mentioned. Dharma is known as a person's purpose in life or role in the Universe, which includes righteousness. Where as a Hindu, I derive my Dharma from my caste (or level of hierarchy in life), as a Buddhist, I derive my Dharma from the teachings of Buddha.

Hindus and Buddhists share a common practice of mantras, although they may use them in slightly different ways. Buddhists use mantras primarily for problem-solving and control of thoughts, while Hindus use mantras primarily for religious rituals and worshiping God.

Both Buddhists and Hindus meditate. While Buddhists use meditation primarily to attain Nirvana, Hindus generally use meditation for physical improvement and spiritual growth. Buddhists believe in one God, whereas Hindus worship many gods. According to a web article in "Asian Highlights," to reach Nirvana (heaven), Buddhists believe in the "Eightfold Path," which consists of right view, right resolve, right speech, right conduct, right livelihood, right effort, right mindfulness, and right Samadhi (Carol).

Some Hindus still follow a caste system, and Buddhists do not. Buddhists believe Siddhartha Gautama Buddha to be the founder of Buddhism. They view him as a great teacher who found enlightenment and founded the Buddhist religion.

There are three branches of Buddhism. These are called Theravada, Mahayana, and Vajrayana. There isn't any recognized Bible of Buddhism, although the Tripitaka is considered a major sacred text. The Tripitaka text and the Pali Canon scriptures are closely related. Other important Buddhist texts include the Chinese Buddhist Canon and the Tibetan Buddhist Canon. All three of the Buddhist branches contain several collections of texts and scriptures that form the doctrine of Buddhist teachings, rules, and devotions (Reiss).

Judaism

I am now a Jewish man living in Israel and speaking Hebrew. Judaism, also known as the Jewish religion, consists of Orthodox Jews, Conservative Jews, and Liberal Jews. The Orthodox Jews believe in heaven and hell. As an Orthodox Jew, I believe in doing good deeds to earn the path to heaven. Good deeds, especially when they help others, are known as "Mitzvahs." Being reverent and treating others well will create multiple Mitzvahs and increase the chances of finding heaven in the Afterlife. Conservative Jews may or may not believe in an Afterlife. Most Liberal Jews do not believe in a life after this one; they believe your physical body returns to the Earth. Descriptions of heaven and hell are somewhat ambiguous in the Jewish scriptures. Heaven may be described as physical pleasures, teachings of the Jewish beliefs, or a Garden of Eden. Hell may be seen as a place to be punished, or as a fiery hell. Jews may believe that their actions on Earth create merits awarded in the Afterlife. They may also believe that judgment does not occur until the Afterlife is reached.

According to an article in the *Jerusalem Post*, "Some rabbis and Jewish people believe the Messiah (God incarnate) will come to Earth, Jesus will return to Israel, and the Jewish people will unite with God" (Weiss). In general, Jews do not believe in multiple Afterlives. In Judaism, Yahweh is the God of Abraham, Isaac, and Jacob. Yahweh is the God of the Israelites, and often, Jews worship the God of Abraham.

The Torah is considered the Hebrew Bible. According to "Bible Reasons," the Torah contains "the five books of Moses: Genesis, Exodus, Leviticus, Numbers, and Deuteronomy. It is, in essence, the Hebrew Bible. It contains 613 Commandments and is the entire context of Jewish laws and traditions. The Jews do not call this the Old Testament because for them, they do not have a New Testament" (Evans). The Talmud is also Hebrew Scripture. The Talmud deciphers and explains the written text of the Torah. It was compiled by many rabbis, but Jews believe it originally came from God.

Islam

I am now living in Iran, and I am a Muslim. Islam is one of the youngest religions in the world. It started in Mecca, in what is now Saudi Arabia, during the life of the prophet Mohammed. Those that believe in the Islamic faith are called Muslims. Most Muslims are monotheistic, and the God they worship is Allah (Tawhid). Muslims believe that Jesus, Abraham, and Moses were all prophets but that Mohammed was the final prophet—and the one that must be worshiped. The Qur'an is the primary holy text of Islam and is believed to be the Word of God. Muslims believe that when they die, Allah will judge them. Where they will reside after death is determined by their behavior while living. Jannah is paradise or the Muslim version of heaven, and they also believe in hell (Jahannam). After death, Muslims may go to "Barzakh," where they await judgment. This holding ground reminds me of the purgatory that Catholics believe in. Virtuous deeds or poor behavior determines my destination of heaven or hell, respectively. According to the BBC, good deeds include worship of Allah, the routine of prayer, helping others, and following the teachings of the Qur'an. ("Akhirah")

There are many other religions in the world, such as Mormonism, Scientology, Jainism, Shinto, and Taoism. To discuss all of these religions would extend beyond the scope of this book.

You and I could have been born into any one of the religions I've mentioned. If we were, we would not have the same religious and spiritual beliefs that we have today. If I were born into Hinduism and raised with this may be why, even among Christians, there are sometimes differing interpretations of specific passages.

It is more important that people believe in God than that they worship in a particular manner. I am also fine with them worshipping "their God," even though I believe there is only one God. It is important for all men and women to lead righteous lives, because a lack of spiritual grace has consequences. The consequences may occur now or in your Afterlife.

As I took a quick synopsis of the major religions of the world, previously described, I found some similarities. Almost all religions believe in heaven and hell. Your destination of heaven versus hell depends upon how you have lived. All religions believe in "cause and effect." Our actions have consequences and determine our eternal future. In Hinduism and Buddhism, this is known as karma. If you live as a righteous person creating good deeds, you go to heaven. If you live as an infamous person and commit bad deeds, you go to hell. For some religions (Judaism, Catholicism, Hinduism), there may be a holding ground prior to a decision being made on your ultimate fate. Usually, this decision is made by God.

I was surprised to learn that multiple Afterlives are a fairly common religious concept, especially for Hindus and Buddhists who believe in reincarnation. My concept of multiple Afterlives is, therefore, not original.

I also found similarities and differences among religions regarding my concept of learning spiritual lessons. Although words referring to spiritual lessons are only sometimes used in other religions, there is the use of synonymous words and phrases. For example, in place of the spiritual lesson of "giving," Judaism replaces giving with the word Mitzvah. Mitzvahs, of course, are good deeds that help others. In several religions, they talk about good deeds, whereas I talk about learning spiritual lessons to reach a better Afterlife.

Most religions believe in a soul and that when you die, your physical body is lost, but your soul lives on. Exceptions are Hinduism and Buddhism, where the belief is that you reincarnate into a new physical body after death. However, you do take your soul with you into the new body.

All religions have either religious scripture, religious texts, or Bibles. Some religions believe this is the direct Word of God, and some do not. When they believe in the Word of God, they believe that God's words are literally transferred to the authors, who then transfer them onto paper. Christians believe the Holy Bible to be the Word of God, and Muslims believe the Qur'an to be the Word of God. The Hindus do not believe their scriptures are the Word of God.

Not all religions worship the same God. For Buddhists, Buddha is their God. For the most part, Judaism, Christianity, and the Islamic faith all worship the God of Abraham. Hindus are principally devoted to the Gods Vishnu, Shiva, and Brahma.

Some religions are more liberal in that they are more tolerant and respectful of other religious beliefs and may even appreciate the differences in religions. Hinduism tends to be relatively more tolerant. Liberal Jews seem to be very tolerant of other people's beliefs and religions. Some religions will accept that there may be more than one way to heaven, and others may not. Christians believe you can only go to heaven if you believe Jesus Christ is the Messiah, and Muslims believe you can only go to heaven as a follower of Allah. I believe that all righteous persons eventually reach heaven. All persons eventually become righteous, but it may take them multiple Afterlives to learn their spiritual lessons and fully practice spiritual virtues.

In history, there have been many religious conflicts, often known as "Holy Wars," among many men of different religions. Many of these disputes have been over land. There were multiple conflicts between Catholics and Protestants in the 16th and 17th centuries in Europe. Israeli and Palestinian conflicts have been ongoing for the past 300 years or so. Religion can bring peace and love to man, but it can also be the cause of intense fighting and death. Tolerance between religions is paramount to grow collective peace and harmony among man. When people are spiritual but not religious, conflict is less likely to be an issue. This is one of the main reasons that I emphasize Divine Energy or God in this book. If we all believe in God and keep our religious beliefs and rituals personal to ourselves, Holy Wars may be avoided. No matter what religion we practice or what spiritual beliefs we have, we must always practice love, kindness, tolerance, and patience with our fellow man.

In general, I have found that religions that believe their Bible is the Word of God are less accepting of different faiths than those religions that believe scriptures are written by men (some prophets) and not by God. The reason is that texts and scripture written by man can be interpreted in different ways, but since Bibles are the Word of God, they are set in stone. When the Bible is taken literally, the Word of God can never be questioned. For those literal believers, God's word was applicable 2,000 years ago, and his word is the same today and forever. For those who do not believe that the Bible is God's absolute word, they encourage people to view each passage according to the relevance of its time in history.

Some religions view Earthly religious leaders as special prophets, while others view these prophets as gods. Whereas Christians believe Christ roamed the Earth as a prophet, he is also viewed as God. Most Jews believe that Jesus Christ was a prophet, but not the Messiah. To Muslims, Allah was both a prophet and their God. Most religions recognize Buddha as a living prophet between 563-483 BCE, but only Buddhists worship him as God.

You will decide for yourself who were prophets and who were also Gods. You will determine through your faith which God(s) you will worship. At this time, there is no universal truth. When you die, you will find the answer in your Afterlife, and the absolute truth will be known to you. The prophets will become less important to you in the Afterlife because the prophets will be One with Almighty God. Salvation and eternal life will be available to all righteous people at some point in time.

The purpose of this chapter was to help you explore your religious and spiritual beliefs. Please examine your spiritual growth. Allow this chapter to bring you closer to God. I plead with and challenge you to lead a spiritual life that is tolerant of all people of the world.

Affirmation: "I acknowledge that to die is to be reborn and to live in bliss for all eternity."

CHAPTER 15
Conclusion: Death and Life's Purpose

Of course, you don't die. Nobody dies. Death doesn't exist. You only reach a new level of vision, a new realm of consciousness, a new unknown world.

—Henry Miller

A Retrospective Look

By imagining my own death, I enhanced and grew many of my current spiritual beliefs found in this book. Although I had an extensive 35–40 year background reading personal growth books, many of these were not spiritual in nature. I realize now that the best and most comprehensive books on personal growth include spiritual life.

I also realize that many personal growth books do not address death or life after death. If they do, little time is devoted to the subject. I find this curious since death is such a big part of all of our lives. I hope that by experiencing your imaginary death and reading about my 'Afterlife,' you will be able to approach your life more positively. I wish that your close examination of your personal death will bring you a wise perspective on the life-death-life continuum. I also trust that you will become more comfortable with your inevitable demise as you improve your understanding of the benefits of your imaginary death, having scrutinized it. An examination of your death always provides the clearest understanding of your life. By reviewing your life's decisions and actions, you can choose to grow your spiritual life and make the world a better place to live.

Before writing this book, I decided to meditate on what my Afterlife would look like. This took a lot of imagination, but to my wonderful surprise, I intuitively sensed with confidence that there was a high degree of truth in my perceptions of the Afterlife. I now have faith that when I leave this world, I will experience many of the events written about in these previous Afterlife descriptions. I feel certain I will rejoin many, if not all, of my dear deceased family members. I feel that I am closer to God than ever before, and that I will be having close communication with Him (or Her) in several future lifetimes before finally joining Him as One. I also feel certain that even though I most likely will have multiple Afterlives, I will never be born again with a physical body. My future lives will consist of my higher consciousness.

Writing this comprehensive book, I was greatly challenged to find the right words, but at the same time, it stimulated my sixth sense and other Spiritual Senses, allowing me to grow exponentially. I would love to see this happen for you as well.

This process has given me:

1. Self-belief.

The writing of this book has given me greater self-belief and self-worth. When I started the exercise of being dead and self-reflecting, I began to feel selfish. However, during my conversation with my mother during my imaginary Afterlife, she reminded me of all my selfless acts during my life. This helped restore my feelings of self-worth.

I also was faced with many failures experienced throughout my life. This reduced my self-esteem. For instance, I questioned whether I was a good father because I hadn't spent enough time with my two sons. I felt that I would have had better relationships with them had I concentrated less on my career. In this way, I thought that many of my precious years were wasted. Eventually, by meditating and contemplating on my relationships with my children, I learned that I had also given them much love when they needed it most. I observed their success and am now beginning to believe that I am at least partially responsible for this.

In my early death meditations, facing my life events was sometimes extremely difficult because it conjured up feelings of inadequacy. Through visualizing my own death during meditation, however, I would eventually realize that I have accomplished many wonderful things in my life, such as a successful medical career, sharing intense love with my family, and learning to give of myself to others. Concentrating on the gifts given to me by the Spiritual Universe has lessened all my self-doubts.

2. A Renewed Spirit

I realized that my bond with God had weakened over the years. No one around me seemed very spiritual anymore, so I didn't see the point of being spiritual myself. My mother was my true friend and spiritual inspiration; after her death, when she was no longer available to discuss spiritual topics, I allowed my spiritual self to become less of a priority.

By performing meditative exercises (with keen awareness) in which I saw myself dead, and by slowly and painstakingly reliving all the details of my life, I refreshed my Spirit and strengthened my relationship with God. Now, I renew my vow to grow my spiritual self as much as possible. I have started to read the Bible again. As I read the Bible and talk with God, I solidify my belief that my purpose in life is to serve God.

3. Selflessness.

I wasn't so selfish after all. I worked in the medical field for forty years and selflessly helped as many patients as I could. I even saved a few lives. For the first time, I became truly aware that removing the malignant melanomas

I had found on patients' skin had probably lengthened or even saved their lives. For the first time, I remembered the time during a routine skin exam in dermatology when I found a lump on a patient's neck and told him to follow up with our head and neck physician to rule out carcinoma. He came back to me the next month, tremendously grateful, because it did turn out to be cancer. He told me he was extremely fortunate that I found it early. It was then removed.

The exercise of imaginary death also made me aware that, although I didn't give my kids as much time as I would've liked, I did give them genuine, unconditional love. I was always there when they really needed me. I realize now that my guidance, given to them over the years, was deeply appreciated, and this reflected the time I took to teach them. For the first time, I became truly aware that I had been a good dad.

Writing this book itself is also a selfless act. I have genuinely written this book in an effort to bring people to God and to help them with their lives. Without meditation, prayer, and God's guidance, this book would probably never have been written. Over the years, many of the personal growth books I read helped me with my flaws and taught me how to be a better person. This has given me the opportunity to share my knowledge with all of you. It is my sincere hope that this book will help you to be a better individual and to live a happier life.

4. Less Fear of Death.

Having experienced death in my imagination, I have become much less fearful of death. I can't say I am 100 percent free of the fear of death, but my fear level has been reduced dramatically. I am also better prepared for my death than ever before. I am in tune with the things I would like to accomplish before my demise. Most of my "bucket list" has already been achieved. When it is my time to cross over to my Afterlife, I don't think I will have any regrets.

5. *Connection with God*

I have reconnected with my spiritual self. My relationship with God and Jesus Christ is stronger than ever. I plan on continuing to work on my life's spiritual lessons. I know that with God at my side, I will be the best person I can be.

6. *More Spirit and Fewer Physical Possessions.*

I am much less centered around achieving money and possessions. I spend more time filling my mind with positive thoughts and spreading spiritual virtues. I am always striving to strengthen my love for my significant other, my sons, my stepdaughter, my siblings, and my family and friends. I treat all of my neighbors in the Universe with respect and love.

The growth of my Spirit is my main priority in life. By working on my spiritual lessons, I try to become one with my soul, which I believe to be my true (authentic) self. My purpose in life is to be in touch with my true, spiritual self, and then utilize this understanding by taking positive action in all of my life's endeavors. By further developing my spiritual awakening to the principles of spiritual development as described in this book, I am hopeful that the rest of my life on Earth will be filled with contentment, peace, and happiness, as I prepare myself to transition to my new Afterlife.

I achieved one of my purposes in life when I discovered that my true self is not my physical shell. Realizing that my true self is my spiritual self, and not my physical body, I have faith that the meaning of life is the realization that humans do not die, but rather, are reborn into the eternity of their Afterlives. Using this knowledge of everlasting life, I make all of my important decisions and actions. Through Universal Wisdom and Spiritual Synchronicity, I trust that my Afterlife will come at the exact right time.

7. Fun, Laughter, and Joy

I am now more fun and laugh more often. I feel more joy than ever before. Recently, my family and I celebrated my sixty-seventh birthday at my condominium, and I created a party game for everyone to play. My family loves to play board games, but I am not a huge fan; therefore, in place of a board game, I decided to create a party game. We all played—many parts of the game were funny, and we laughed a lot. After the game, my son Adam said that he thought my creation of a party game was the result of my recent retirement. I thought about what he said. His words were true, but there was much more behind the party game's creation than simply my retirement. Because I had been writing this book, I was conscious of my spiritual virtues and spiritual lessons on a daily basis. Every day, I was practicing being kind and sensitive to the needs of others. It was important for me to spread love during all my person-to-person encounters. During the day, if a negative thought about someone entered my ego mind, I would immediately stop that thought and switch my thinking to a productive idea. My kindness, love for my family, and improved creativity and imagination (or developed Spiritual Senses) led to the fun party game. This game would not have been created if it were not for my pursuit of spiritual growth.

Throughout my life, I have had a moderate temper and have been known to lose my patience. Unfortunately, my sons have always been aware of this. I am now developing more patience and a softer disposition as I awaken my internal Spirit. My increased creativity and kindness can be traced to my awareness and performance of my spiritual virtues and my spiritual lessons. A greater awareness of my eventual death has sparked a desire to have fun. I enjoy it when I am funny and love to laugh with my family and others. Through my spiritual awakening, I have learned that the love I receive from my family and the Divine Universe are rewarding me with true riches. Happiness occurs when we have fun with family and friends. When we smile and laugh, we find deep joy.

As I experience activities and interactions that I am passionate about, I receive from the Universe a deep sense of fulfillment. This fulfillment results in my joy. I am now rich. If you want success in life, discover what makes you happy. Follow your heart's desire and all your passions. Find true riches instead of monetary wealth. Use the spiritual virtues listed in this book and the described spiritual lessons as a stepping-stone to laughter and fun. Spread kindness and love to manifest deep joy. This is what I am doing.

A Quick Review of Some Key Points

1. Your physical body is not who you are. You are a spiritual entity trapped in a physical body.

2. You are here to connect with Divine Energy or God.

3. Your Crossover to your Afterlife is sooner than you think.

4. Believe that death is a chance to be reborn into a better consciousness.

5. Believe through faith that you will reach the Kingdom of Heaven by living virtuously.

6. Be kind, giving, honest, and tolerant.

7. Use God's assistance to think positively and to create wonderful out comes.

8. Learn to meditate your own way.

9. Consider meditating on your imaginary death. This will help you to understand who you are and how to live.

10. Become Spiritually Balanced for a successful and happy life.

11. Remove self-doubts by focusing on your accomplish-ments. Appreciate the gifts God has given you instead of focusing on your inadequacies.

12. Practice using your higher consciousness to become a powerful problem solver. This will connect you to Universal Wisdom and Divine Energy.

13. Find the synchronicities in your life, and you will see God's plan for you.

14. See the Oneness in your life and the Universe around you.

15. Develop your intuition and clairvoyance to keep yourself safe and to anticipate life-changing events.

16. Keep yourself physically, mentally, and spiritually healthy.

17. Love yourself, your family, your neighbors, and God with all your heart.

18. Happiness occurs when we have no regrets. We are as happy as we make up our minds to be.

19. Religion is faith and not fact.

20. God and Jesus Christ are our ticket to eternity.

21. Live like you are dying.

What can this book do for you?

This book should be used as an impetus to begin or strengthen your spiritual journey. This book can also be used as a practical guide. Hopefully, you have read this book in its entirety. Reflect on your life and imaginary death so you can learn from it. By connecting with your inevitable death, it will be easier to understand the life you have lived. When you genuinely believe that your next life (Afterlife) and its spiritual level is determined by your goodness and Spirit in this lifetime, you will live with supreme spiritual virtues and pristine moral values. Your actions in this life will determine your degree of happiness in your next life. It is of paramount importance not to miss this opportunity.

Face all the past, present, and future events in your lifetime. Examine death closely until you can see it, embrace it, learn from it, and prepare for it. Believe in your heart that death and life are the same thing. When our flesh dies, our new life becomes even more wondrous than this one. Gaining blissful eternity is far better than being trapped in a decaying body. Use your newfound perspective on death to awaken your spiritual journey. Your imaginary death should be utilized to appreciate your Godlike Spirit. Allow this death to teach you a better way to live now. Spread your kindness and love to the Universe, and the Divine Universe will give you fun, laughter, and joy.

Develop your Spiritual Senses of creativity, awareness, intuition, insight, and imagination to bring more fun, laughter, and joy into your life. Spreading kindness, love, and joy to the Divine Universe will prepare you to receive even greater riches in your next life.

I am hopeful that by the words and messages in this book, you will be able to live a fulfilling and joyous life by zeroing in on your own personal spiritual development. By utilizing the process of visualizing and then experiencing your own death, you will learn the best ways to live. By looking back on your life, you may think of all your fantastic achievements and accomplishments. With reflection and keen awareness, you will remember all the little miracles you created but have forgotten.

Realize that, like George Bailey, you have affected many lives in wondrous ways. In the movie, It's a Wonderful Life, Clarence (my friend), George's guardian angel, showed George that if he had never lived, the lives of friends and family members in the town of Bedford Falls would have been disastrous. George learned that he had a positive impact on so many lives. He was previously unaware of all the wonderful things he had done for folks. He had even saved his brother's life by pulling him out of the broken ice. If it were not for George, the town of Bedford Falls would have fallen under the control of the devious Mr. Potter, thereby succumbing to ruin and financial disaster. George only learns to appreciate and become grateful for his life by experiencing a fallen Bedford Falls in which he was never born. He now genuinely appreciates living with his wife, Mary, and their kids. He becomes thankful for having the job at the old Bailey Building and Loan, one that he earlier wanted so much to escape from. We, like George, only appreciate all the lives we impact when we imagine our death.

Can we more fully appreciate our lives by experiencing our own deaths? Can we appreciate our own death by seeing it as new life? This book makes the case that we can. It is through dying that we learn how to live. Dying is a spiritual event, and so is living. We are not simply "of the flesh." Our true authentic selves consist of a spiritual soul created by a Divine Energy Source or God. If we develop our Godlike Divine Universal Energy while we are still alive, we will experience love and find our true purpose for living. We will find happiness, become less fearful of death, and look forward to everlasting life.

Affirmation: "I will live righteously because actions have consequences in this lifetime and the lifetimes to come."

Works Cited

"Akhirah - Muslim beliefs – GCSE Religious Studies Revision." BBC, 2021, bbc.co.uk/bitesize/guide/z43pfew/revision/5.

"Asceticism." New World Encyclopedia, 7 Nov 2021, 13:22 UTC. 4 Nov 2022, 13:28 https://www.newworldencyclopedia.org/p/index.php? title=Asceticism&oldid=1059936.

Ben-Shahar, Tal. Happier. McGraw Hill, 2007.

Berman, David. "The Ten Dimensions of String Theory." Plus. Maths.org., 9 Oct. 2012, Plus.maths.org/content/10-dimensions-and-more-string-theory.

Bernstein, Gabrielle. May Cause Miracles. 2nd ed., Harmony Books, 2013.

Canfield, Jack, et.al., The Power of Focus. 10th anniversary ed., Health Communications, 2011.

Carnegie, Dale. How to Win Friends & Influence People. Pocket Books, 4th ed., 1982.

Carol. "Hinduism Vs Buddhism-3 Major Similarities and 7 Major differences." Asia Highlights. 09 June 2022, Asiahighlights.com/india/Hinduism/-vs-buddhism.

Chatel, Amanda. "What 7 Religions Think Happens After You Die." Bustle, 22 Dec. 2014, https://www.bustle.com/articles/55208-do-hindus-believe-in-heaven-what-7-major-religions-believe-about-death-and-the-afterlife.

Cherry, Kendra. "Taking the Steps to Forgive Yourself." Verywellmind, 17 Feb. 2021, verywellmind.com/how-to-forgive-yourself-4583819.

"What is a Guilt Complex" Verywellmind, 21 Aug. 2022, verywellmind.com/guilt-complex-definition-symptoms traits-causes-treatment-5115946.

Chopra, Deepak. The Book of Secrets: Unlocking the Hidden Dimensions of Your Life. 2nd ed., Three Rivers Press, 2004.

Common English Bible, Christian Resources Development Corporation, 2011.

Dooley, Mike. Infinite Possibilities. The Art of Your Living Dreams. 10th anniversary ed., Atria Paperback, 2019.

Dream Team. "Personal Agency: The Art of Making Empowering Choices that are True to You." Remi (Sharon) Pearson, 26 Jul. 2019, remipearson.com/post/personal-agency.

Dyer, Saje and Serena Dyer Pisoni. The Knowing: Eleven Lessons to Understand the Quiet Urges of Your Soul, Sounds True, 2021.

Dyer, Wayne W. Change Your Thoughts-Change Your Life: Living the Wisdom of the Tao. Hay House, 2007.

---. The Power of Intention: Learning to Co-Create Your World Your Way. 2nd ed., Hay House, 2011.

---. There's a Spiritual Solution to Every Problem. 2nd ed., HarperCollins Publishers, 2003.

---. Wishes Fulfilled: Mastering the Art of Manifesting. 6th ed., Hay House, 2013.

---. You'll See it When you Believe it: The Way to your Personal Transformation. 2nd ed., HarperCollins Publishers, 2001.

---. There's a Spiritual Solution to too Every Problem. 2nd ed., HarperCollins Publishers, 2003.

Evans, Ashley. "Talmud vs. Torah," Bible Reasons, 5 June 2022, Biblereasons.com/Talmud-vs-torah.

factsanddetails.com. "Maharishi, Mahesh Yogi, Transcendental Meditation and the Beatles." factsanddetails.com. Sept. 2018, https://factsanddetails.com/india/Religion_Caste_Folk_Beliefs_Death/sub7_2d/entry-5638.html.

"H. Jackson Brown Quotes". Goodreads. Goodreads, 2022, Goodreads.com/author/quotes/33394.H_Jackson_Brown_Jr_

Hill, Napoleon. Think & Grow Rich. Rev. ed., Fawcett Crest, 1963.

Hill, Napoleon and W. Clement Stone. Success Through a Positive Mental Attitude. 2nd ed., Pocket Books, 1977.

History.com Editors. "Islam – Five Pillars, Nation of Islam & Definition History." History.com, 20 Aug. 2019, history.com/topics/religion/islam.

Hoge, Elizabeth, et al. "Controlled Trial of Mindfulness, Meditation for General Anxiety Disorder: Effects on Anxiety and Stress Reactivity." Journal of Clinical Psychology, vol. 74, no. 8, Aug. 2013, pp. 786-792. https://doi.org/10.4088%2FJCP.12m08083.

Hopcke, Robert H. There are No Accidents: Synchronicity and the Stories of Our Lives. 2nd ed., Riverhead Books, July 1998.

It's a Wonderful Life. Directed by Frank Capra, performances by James Stewart, Donna Reed, RKO Radio Pictures, 1946.

Izzo, John. The Five Secrets You Must Discover Before You Die. Berrett-Koehler Publishers, 2008.

"Karma and Reincarnation." Hinduism Today, 5 Sept. 2019, https://www.hindu-ismtoday.com/hindu-basics/karma-and-reincarnation/.

Kirshenbaum, Mira. Everything Happens for a Reason: Finding the True Reason for the Events in Our Lives. MJF Books / Crown Publishing Group, 2004.

Lennon, John. "Imagine." Apple Records, AZzlyrics.com,1971, azlyrics.com/lyrics/johnlennon/imagine.html.

Le Shan, Lawrence. How to Meditate. 2nd ed., Bantam Books, 1975.

Lester, Meera. The Law of Attraction Made Easy. Adams Media, 2016.

 Likurlansik, Stuart L. and Mario Maffei. "Somatic Symptom Disorder." American Family Physician, vol. 93, no. 1, Jan. 2016, pp. 49-54A. https://www.aafp.org/pubs/afp/issues/2016/0101/p49.html.

Love, Lisa. "The Spiritual Use of the Law of Attraction." Daily Om, Accessed 08 2022, dailyom.com/cgi-bin/display/librarydisplay.cgi?lid=1317.

Marshall, Collin. "What is Higher Consciousness?: How We Can Transcend our Petty Day-to-Day Desires and Gain a Deeper Wisdom." OPEN CULTURE, 25 Nov. 2019, https://www.openculture.com/2019/11/what-is-higher-consciousness.html.

Matsumoto, Yui, et. al. "Transcriptome Characterization of Reverse Development Turritopsis dohrnii (Hydrozoa Cnidaria)." G3: Genes/Genomes/Genetics, vol. 9, no. 12, 2019, pp. 4127-4138. https://doi.org/10.1534/g3.119.400487.

Maltz, Maxwell. Psycho-Cybernetics. Updated and expanded ed., Penguin Random House, Nov. 2015.

Mayo Clinic Staff. "Living Wills and Advance Directives for Medical Decisions." Mayo Clinic, 02 Aug. 2020, https://www.mayoclinic.org/healthy-lifestyle/consumer-health/in-depth/living-wills/art-20046303.

New World Encyclopedia. Ascetism. New World Encyclopedia, 7 Nov. 2021, https://www.newworldencyclopedia.org/p/index.php? title=Ascetism&ol-did=1059936.

Noonan, Michael. "Moksha in Hinduism: Overview & Stages." Study.Com, 27 Feb. 2022, https://study.com/academy/lesson/moksha-in-hinduism-definition-les-son-quiz.html.

Olsson, Regan. "8 Ways to Take Care of Your Spiritual Health." Banner Health, 26 June 2021, https://www.bannerhealth.com/healthcareblog/better-me/8-ways-to-take-care-of-your-spiritual-health.

Peale, Norman Vincent. The Power of Positive Thinking. 1st ed., A Touchstone Book, 2015.

Perry, Elizabeth. "Overcome Self-Doubt (Once and For All) 8 Tips to Move Forward." Betterup.com, 11 Feb. 2022, betterup.com/blog/overcoming-self-doubt.

"Power of Attorney." ABA, 2002, https://www.americanbar.org/groups/real_prop-erty_trust_estate/resources/estate_planning/power_ of_ attorney/.

Pueblo, Yung. Inward. Andrews McMeel Publishing, 2018.

Quinn, Ariel. "Spiritual Balance and 8 Tips for Finding it." Herway.net, 2 Mar. 2022, herway.net/spiritual-balance/.

Rahul. "Concept of God in Hinduism." Hinduism Facts, 12 Aug. 2021, https://www.hinduismfacts.org/concept-of-god-in-hinduism/.

Reiss, John. "Sacred Texts of Buddhism: What is the Tripitaka?" Study.com, 27 February 2022, https://study.com/academy/lesson/the-three-baskets-and-the-dham-mapada-description-overview.html.

Singer, Michael A. The Untethered Soul: The Journey Beyond Yourself. New Harbinger Publications / Noetic Books, 2007.

Solomon, Prashant. "The Balance of Life." The Daily Guardian, 11 Jan. 2021, thedailyguardian.com/the-balance-of-life/.

Strong, Danny, creator. Levinson, Barry, creator. "Dopesick." Hulu TV Series, Performance by Michael Keaton et al., Hulu streaming, 13 Oct. 2021-17 Nov. 2021, last of 8 episodes, Hulu.com/video/Dopesick.

"Synchronicity." Merriam-Webster.com Dictionary, Merriam-Webster, https://www.merriam- webster.com/dictionary/synchronicity, Accessed 24 Jul. 2022.

"Synchronicity." Wikipedia, The Free Encyclopedia, 10 Sept. 2022, en.wikipedia. org/wiki/Synchronicity#cite_note-kerr2013-1, No changes made.

Taibbi, Robert. "Irrational Guilt: How to Put it to Rest." Psychology Today, 19 Feb. 2016, psychologytoday.com/us/blog/fixing-families/201602/irrational-guilt-how-put-it-rest#.

The Holy Bible. New Living Translation, Tyndale House Publishers, 2015.

Tolle, Eckhart. The Power of Now: A Guide to Spiritual Enlightenment. 2nd ed., Namaste Publishing / New World Library, Sept. 2004.

Vaz, Ronsley. "The Connection Between Freedom and Happiness." Amplify, https://mustamplify.com/the-connection-between-freedom-and-happiness/.   Accessed 08 Aug. 2022.

Wachs, Kate. Love Secrets: Solving the Mysteries of the Love Cycle. Paper Chase Press, 2000.

Warren, Rick. The Purpose Driven Life. 3rd ed., Zondervan, 2012.

Walsch, Neale Donald. What God Said. Penguin Group, 2013.

Weiss, Stewart. "What Jews believe about the afterlife?" The Jerusalem Post, vol. 19, no. 21, 16 Dec.2021, Jpost.com/Judaism/what-do-jews-believe-about-the-afterlife-688956.

Wikipedia contributors. "Buddhist texts." Wikipedia, The Free Encyclopedia. Wikipedia, The Free Encyclopedia, 17 Oct. 2022. Web. 8 Nov. 2022, en.wikipedia. org/wiki/Buddhist_ texts.

Williamson, Marianne. A Return to Love: Reflections on the Principles of a Course in Miracles. 1st ed., HarperOne, 2012.

Wilson, Liz. "Buddhism and Ascetism " Oxford Bibliographies, 18 Aug. 2021, https://www.oxfordbibliographies.com/view/document/obo-9780195393521/obo-9780195393521-0206.xml.

Wright, Vinita Hampton. "The Spiritual Meaning of Balance." Ignatian Spirituality, 2016, ignatianspirituality.com/the-spiritual-meaning-of-balance/.

Zukav, Gary. The Seat of the Soul. 25th anniversary ed., Simon & Schuster Paperbacks, 2014.

Live Like You Are Dying

About the Author

Michael Tortorello writes about modern-day spiritual concepts and poignant personal growth ideas. His creative combination of both fiction and non-fiction produces fun fantasy while teaching life's important spiritual lessons.

As a physician assistant and passionate reader, Michael has studied the subjects of self-help, spirituality, and religion for forty years. By operating on heart patients and treating skin cancers, he has gained a unique perspective on serious illness and death.

This spiritual book, Live Like You Are Dying, will inspire you to connect with Divine Universal Energy to find success and victory in both your life and your Afterlife.